"These wise and compassionate trainings teach us how to access our inner strength, creativity, and love—awakening the deep and lasting well-being we most long for."

—**Tara Brach**, author of *Radical Acceptar*
Radical Compassion

"Glassman's program gives us a clear pathway to seeing the good in ourselves, in others, and in the world around us. All of us could benefit from reading this book. It is truly transformative!"

—**Hal Elrod**, international keynote speaker, and best-selling author of *The Miracle Morning* and *The Miracle Equation*

"This wonderful book shows you how to use practical daily exercises based on the science of positive psychology to enrich your life."

—**Alan Carr, PhD**, professor of clinical psychology at University College Dublin, and author of *Positive Psychology and You*

"We are living in a time of great uncertainty, environmental crisis, and dramatically increased stress. The ocean of our collective minds is in turmoil. In this book, Glassman provides a lighthouse for us; a place of sanctuary, where we can swim out of the rough sea and find a place of humor, joy, and playfulness. A place where we can find our true nature once again."

—**Craig Foster**, naturalist/filmmaker, producer of the Oscar-winning *My Octopus Teacher*, coauthor of *Underwater Wild*, and cofounder of the Seachange project

"Open, accessible, and filled with meaningful exercises to help the reader discover a reliable path toward the positive in life, *A Happier You* skillfully delivers on what it promises."

—**Zindel Segal, PhD**, coauthor of *The Mindful Way through Depression*

"In *A Happier You*, Scott Glassman teaches you how to skillfully focus on the joyful and meaningful moments that are hiding in plain sight—and how to find the happiness strategies that best fit you."

—**Nataly Kogan**, author of *Happier Now*, and founder of Happier, Inc.

"In these crazy times, we all need more resilience, and we all need ways to access the peace and joy that is always within our grasp—regardless of outer circumstances. Scott Glassman's systematic, evidence-based, and eminently practical program is a veritable toolbox for building a solid life structure in which happiness can flourish, whether the road at the moment is smooth or bumpy."

—**Philip Goldberg**, public speaker; podcast host; and author of numerous books, including *American Veda* and *Spiritual Practice for Crazy Times*

"As opposed to a one-size-fits-all strategy, Glassman provides a multidimensional approach to happiness using gratitude, strengths, humor, kindness, and love to shift your mindset to positive. *A Happier You* offers practical ways to improve multiple domains of your well-being and the lives of people around you, which is both timely and vital."

—**Shawn Achor**, *New York Times* bestselling author of *Big Potential*

A Happier You

A **7**-Week Program to
Transform Negative Thinking
into Positivity & Resilience

Scott Glassman, PsyD

New Harbinger Publications, Inc.

Publisher's Note

Distributed in Canada by Raincoast Books

A HAPPIER YOU is a registered trademark of Scott Glassman

NEW HARBINGER PUBLICATIONS is a registered trademark of
New Harbinger Publications, Inc.

Copyright © 2021 by Scott Glassman
        New Harbinger Publications, Inc.
        5674 Shattuck Avenue
        Oakland, CA 94609
        www.newharbinger.com

The exercise "Treating Yourself" in Week 1 of this program is loosely adapted from the "Raisin Exercise" in MINDFULNESS-BASED COGNITIVE THERAPY FOR DEPRESSION by Zindel V. Segal, J. Mark G. Williams, and John D. Teasdale. Copyright © 2013 Guilford Publications. Used by permission of Guilford Publications.

Cover design by Sara Christian; Acquired by Jess O'Brien; Edited by Teja Watson

---

Library of Congress Cataloging-in-Publication Data on file

Names: Glassman, Scott, author.
Title: A happier you : a seven-week program to transform negative thinking into
    positivity and resilience / by Scott Glassman, PsyD.
Description: Oakland, CA : New Harbinger Publications, Inc., [2021] | Includes
    bibliographical references.
Identifiers: LCCN 2021023031 | ISBN 9781684037858 (trade paperback)
Subjects: LCSH: Happiness. | Negativism. | Resilience (Personality trait)
Classification: LCC BF575.H27 G53 2021 | DDC 158--dc23
LC record available at https://lccn.loc.gov/2021023031

Printed in the United States of America

23   22   21

10   9   8   7   6   5   4   3   2   1   First Printing

Contents

Acknowledgments

This book would not have been possible if it wasn't for the support of the Philadelphia College of Osteopathic Medicine and Independence Blue Cross Foundation in developing the A Happier You program. I am immensely grateful to Dr. Barbara Golden, Dr. Harry Morris, Dr. Robert DiTomasso, Dr. Lisa Corbin, Christina Mazzella, and Deketa Cobb at PCOM for their continuous encouragement along this journey.

I want to acknowledge Dr. Jeff Huffman for his input into the collection of positivity themes incorporated into the program, as well as Benjamin Barnes and Peer Mugnier for their insightful contributions to the original modules. Dr. Josephine Shih has been an inspiring research collaborator as we work toward a clearer understanding of the program's impact on well-being. Along the way, Amanda Alston's research assistance has been another gift.

I owe an enormous debt of gratitude to all those who carefully detailed their inner experiences of positivity for this book, including Greg Castro, Adina Bitner, Janessa Brown, Christine Wilkinson, Silina Flacks, Maya Ehikhamenor, Alyson Zerbe, Nikki Ryan, Anthony Austin, Jonathan Kline, Douglas J. Koch, Brenda Hoffman, Maricela Montijo, Kevin A. Barry, and Faith Tanner. I am especially honored by the dedication and positive spirit that Nikki, Janessa, Maya, and Alyson have brought to their roles as trainers. They have spent many hours teaching Happier You skills in masterful ways.

I am deeply appreciative for everyone at New Harbinger Publications who has shaped and steered this project, including Dorothy Smyk, Wendy Millstine, Jess O'Brien, Vicraj Gill, and T. R. Watson. An author couldn't have asked for a more caring team.

Finally, I want to thank my wife, Linda, and son, Zach, for their love and weekly sacrifices of family time as I wrote. They are the truest reflection of what positive living is, and they make everything else possible, simply by being who they are.

Introduction

We are living in a time of great uncertainty and turmoil. The world seems to constantly pull us away from ourselves, with stressful events, negative thoughts, and upsetting feelings. For many of us, this wave of negativity begins not long after waking up.

Your first thought may be, *Today is going to be overwhelming.* When your phone buzzes with another work-related text message, you might think, *Here comes another problem. And I can't respond right now even though it's urgent.* Say you suddenly remember, then, that you didn't wheel the recycling bin down to the curb. You can feel your anxiety rising. You think, *I'm a disorganized mess.* The negative narrator in your head continues: *It's only Monday! How am I ever going to get through the week? What's the point of trying?* By now, you are seriously considering climbing back into bed.

When consumed by this kind of negative thinking, we enjoy life less, struggle in our relationships, sleep poorly, feel drained, and find it more difficult to remember things (Fredman Stein, Morys-Carter, and Hinkley 2018; Zawadzki, Sliwinski, and Smyth 2018). We become more susceptible to anxiety, depression, and anger. This downward spiral into negativity can leave little room for taking care of yourself at a time when you need it most.

The good news is that you picked up this book. You know that something has to change and, more important, that it *can* change. Something has told you that it is time to start listening more carefully to what you need. Maybe that involves eating a proper meal, spending time with friends, watching a favorite TV show, getting a haircut, or planning to get a good night's sleep. The mere fact that you have read this far suggests you are ready to begin finding the positive side of life more consistently.

A Happier You is your ticket to putting yourself first and feeling more joy and meaning on your life's journey. This program was developed to help you prioritize yourself again, and to do it in a way that better insulates you from stress—whether you want to manage chronic unhappiness, keep negative events from overwhelming you, or learn some extra ways to feel good.

This seven-week guided journey is rooted in the evidence-based principles of positive psychology, the study of optimal living, and offers a variety of positive practices that you can immediately incorporate into your daily routine. You will be led through carefully designed activities that can kick-start your positivity engine and make you more resilient in difficult moments.

You will learn how to spotlight what makes you feel good on a daily basis, and will get to know your best possible self at a deeper level. You will begin experiencing the world in ways that put you in the driver's seat of your emotional well-being. This includes exploring practices like mindfulness, gratitude, humor, and kindness, which research has found can improve your mood (Hendriks et al. 2020; Zhao et al. 2019).

By adding new positive exercises into your routine each week, you will find yourself naturally leaning *away* from the negative and *toward* the good things in life. A Happier You builds this "positivity reflex." Picking up this book is, in itself, a form of self-care. It means you want to get more consistently in touch with your strengths and possibilities.

The first step in our journey together begins with becoming more aware of what you are thinking and feeling. How about we start right now? Let's pause a moment and see where you are emotionally, by answering the following questions:

- Can you think of a few things that have made you happy recently? Or does the past week or two seem pretty dark?

- At what point in your life were you happiest? And why?

- Do you see yourself as a positive or negative person? Regardless of what you think, what would others say?

How did it feel answering these questions? This kind of self-reflection can be challenging, especially if you are struggling with chronic sadness or anxiety. We all confront ups and downs in life, and sometimes many more downs than ups. But believe it or not, you have already begun to take control of your happiness by asking these questions. You stepped back to look at the landscape of your mind, which opens the door to new choices and insights.

For example, maybe you discovered that you are happiest when you are talking to people, versus in a room by yourself. Maybe others see you as happy-go-lucky, but you often feel down inside. Hold on to these revelations. They are precious.

As we travel together through these next seven weeks, one thing is certain: you can expect to have many more revelations. We will move slowly and compassionately, together, throughout this journey. It is also important that we move at a pace that is right for you. I want you to feel encouraged every step along the way as you reveal and create positive experiences.

In my son's elementary school, "bucket-filling" is a way of encouraging good acts. Students can fill their bucket by doing something nice for someone, showing a strength, or achieving something. Often, they are filling someone else's bucket at the same time. These positive choices are celebrated by the addition of brightly colored balls into containers tacked to the wall.

It may help to begin to think of your life as a bucket that you can either fill with positive content, or deplete by focusing on the negative. You might actually want to start trying this method of tracking how you feel right now. Find a clear container, and fill it with some colorful objects when you experience moments that make you feel good. You can add or remove some of the objects each day, depending on how that day went. If you prefer, you could rate your sense of well-being on a scale of 1 to 10, keeping track of how the number changes as you move through the program.

Seeing your bucket level or rating gives you a visual reminder of where you are emotionally. This is great preparation for our work together, which will teach you how to "catch" positive experiences and expand their effect on your day. It also can help you become a sharper observer of your inner self.

Along with watching your inner world, there is a special point of view I hope you will take when exploring A Happier You. I call it "The Flower Philosophy of Change."

The Flower Philosophy of Change

No particular age, race, gender, educational background, life experience, personality trait, or any other personal attribute is required to become a more resilient person who can feel joy and meaning every day. We already have that potential within us.

Think about where flowers come from. A seed placed in the earth already has 98 percent of everything it needs to become that beautiful bloom. In a miraculous way, the blossom's color, pattern, and height already reside within the seed. The only missing ingredients are water, sunlight, and soil—in other words, the right environment for it to reach its full potential.

In A Happier You, I see people in the same way, as naturally prepared to flourish under the right conditions. You already have within you everything you need to grow in positive directions. The skills you learn will act like the water, sunlight, and soil.

Remember how you learned to ride a bicycle? You probably had that ability already present and waiting to jump out of you. However, you needed the right things: a bicycle; a flat, open area; a desire to learn;

someone to show you how to balance; encouragement to keep trying when you fell; and even the right kind of weather. Although these were important supports, none of them by themselves could have resulted in you learning to ride a bike. It only clicked when you were nurtured in many different ways, inside and out.

Finding more consistent happiness depends on the same gentle nourishment, drawn from a number of different sources. Each week focuses on a different source:

Week 1: Positive events

Week 2: Strengths and successes

Week 3: Gratitude

Week 4: Laughter and playfulness

Week 5: Enjoyable and meaningful activities

Week 6: Kindness

Week 7: Love

I know what you may be thinking—flowers need a lot of sunlight and water, and a lot of days those nutrients seem pretty hard to find. You are absolutely right! There are some days that just wear you out. You may feel more like a drooping weed than a vibrant flower.

Here is where you need the compassionate, caring gardener within you the most. Part of the flower philosophy is weathering the stormy, negative days so that you can get back to the sunlight. How exactly is that done? By cultivating acceptance and patience.

I would be setting you up for disappointment if I told you that once you try a new exercise, like catching positive events in Week 1 or writing a gratitude letter in Week 3, that you would have unlimited access to positivity. You will still hit the down notes. Bad things will happen, and they'll get you down. Negative feelings will inevitably appear, along with the brighter ones.

What is important to remember is that negative feelings are not bad, wrong, or shameful. Nowhere in A Happier You do I say that you need to avoid or reject difficult emotions. The intention is not for you to develop a fear of negativity. Feeling sad, angry, and helpless at times is a normal part of life, especially when things happen that are bigger than any of us can control.

The concept of "yin and yang," which comes from the ancient Chinese religious tradition of Taoism, suggests that negative and positive sides of life are necessary parts of being human. In fact, they depend on one another. Happiness would lose its meaning if sadness did not exist.

Before moving ahead, why don't we take a breather, to really take these ideas in.

- Like a flower, you have the built-in potential to bloom, given the right conditions.

- A Happier You gives you a weekly road map, showing you different ways to create those conditions.

- You can't rush a flower into existence—there will be stormy days without sunlight.

- It is perfectly normal to experience down times. In fact, they make the up times more meaningful.

- Meeting negative emotions with acceptance is an important part of well-being.

I should also mention that negative feelings can be useful in a practical sense. Anxiety can motivate you to work harder in some situations (Strack et al. 2017). Anger can generate the energy and persistence needed to remove obstacles standing in the way of your goals (Schmitt, Gielnik, and Seibel 2019). Sadness may lead you to find support for a loss, or create the space you need to recover (Martínez-Hernáez et al. 2016). So there is even an upside to negativity! It all comes down to how we respond to what we feel, what we think, and our circumstances.

Do note, though, that negative thoughts and feelings present a problem when they become overwhelming for long periods of time. If negative thoughts and feelings are disrupting your life in a severe and persistent way, please contact a licensed mental health practitioner or seek an evaluation at a hospital.

If the flower philosophy teaches us anything, it's that even at the worst times, something in you wants to keep growing toward the light. The hope is that this book will be your compassionate guide, always available to you, resting by your side, ready to nourish you and protect you from the elements. A Happier You encourages a "whole self" approach to wellness and self-care.

The Whole Self

Feeling good can come from a variety of sources, like many streams coming together to create a wide river of well-being. They include the seven sources you will explore over the course of this book: positive events, strengths and successes, gratitude, laughter and playfulness, enjoyable and meaningful activities, kindness, and love. What is wonderful about these sources is that each can flow through all aspects of being— emotional, psychological, social, physical, and spiritual—filling the whole self.

How can a single source, like gratitude, have such a far-ranging effect? To understand this better, let's conduct a three-step thought experiment:

Step 1: Think of something you feel grateful for.

Step 2: Ask yourself, what other good thoughts and feelings go along with that gratitude?

Step 3: Ask yourself, has this source of gratitude ever strengthened your connection with others, helped you feel good physically, or given you any emotional or spiritual sustenance?

Nikki, someone experienced with the positivity skills of A Happier You, thought about a video call from her five-year-old nephew. She felt grateful for being the special person that he'd called. He showed her his dance moves during the call, which led to feelings of joy, love, and connection. This single source of thankfulness filled her entire being. She felt more relaxed and connected to her higher power as a result. Gratitude is a way Nikki cares for her whole self every day.

Over the course of this book, you too will learn how to let positivity sources like gratitude flow into different parts of your life experience. The more often you invite these streams in, the better you'll feel and the more resilient you'll become.

You might have picked up this book already knowing which side of yourself needs a boost. You may, for example, feel a social emptiness. In that case, as you move through the weeks of A Happier You, you could:

- Call to mind things that others like about you (Week 2: Strengths)

- Channel thankfulness for positive conversations in the past (Week 3: Gratitude)

- Search for funny things that make you laugh and share them (Week 4: Playfulness)

- Plan a fun or meaningful activity with someone you care about (Week 5: Enjoyable and Meaningful Activities)

As Nikki's example demonstrates, your positivity sources and whole self are interconnected at deep levels. By the end of these next seven weeks, I expect that you will be better able to nourish every dimension of who you are by regularly accessing these sources.

The exercises in this book can also help you find deeper meaning in life. You may now see going to a restaurant with friends simply as a fun outing. After taking a deep dive into that activity, you may also realize how it elevates your social self-care, helps you shake off small stresses, energizes your body, and stimulates awareness of your best qualities. A Happier You will show you how thinking, feeling, and doing get lifted up together. It will teach you how to start and extend these positive chain reactions.

In addition to putting you in touch with self-nurturance and helping you use your whole self, this book will take you back to some of the best aspects of childhood. A *Happier You* gives you permission to be a kid again. Let's take a look at how that will work.

Bringing Out Your Inner Child

While many of us, unfortunately, have experienced difficult or traumatic childhoods, children generally seem to have an easier time feeling happy than adults do. My ten-year-old reminds me of this every time he gets excited about eating a chocolate brownie, and I think, *Wow, if only I got that excited every time I drove to work.*

When you think about becoming your best self, it may help to go back in time and remember the simple pleasures that sparked your enthusiasm, joy, and laughter—those jumping-up-and-down excitements scattered throughout your day.

When you invite your inner child to the table of self-transformation, it means you more fully appreciate having fun and being present. Can you think of the last time you felt like a kid? What were you doing? Who were you with?

Whether you were running through a sprinkler or swinging on a play-ground, it probably involved letting go of worry. The popularity of adult coloring books, social painting nights, and escape rooms shows just how many of us feel that urge to strip away the complications and stress of being adults. The bucket-filling approach to mood awareness is another example of that.

But bringing out the child within doesn't only involve having fun. Your inner child also has a more direct connection to love. Indeed, some research finds that young children build friendships mostly through showing affection (Howes 2009). Love seems woven into our beings at a young age.

Many parts of this book will feature an activity to bring out the "child mind," as a way of supporting your foundation of positivity. These exercises will involve a physical, hands-on activity, such as finding a rock that represents one of your strengths. If you have kids or work with them, you could even invite them to participate in these exercises along with you.

On the other hand, if you do not feel comfortable slipping back into "child mind," that is perfectly okay. There will be plenty of alternatives. The Happier You approach emphasizes creativity, flexibility, and choice, versus one-size-fits-all.

How to Use This Book

Improving your quality of life in a significant and lasting way takes practice. Each chapter contains a week's worth of practice, with an assortment of exercises to try. Positivity is a skill, and like any skill, the more you practice the better you get!

Just like learning to ride a bike, A Happier You takes a step-by-step approach to making positivity more automatic. It requires patience, persistence, and a willingness to try new things. I also suggest setting aside about fifteen to thirty minutes a day for the full seven weeks of the program.

As I mentioned earlier, each of the seven weeks will focus on a different positivity source, or Core Positivity Practice. Let's have another look at this road map, viewed through this lens, to see where we are headed together:

Week 1: Catching Positive Events

Week 2: Exploring Successes and Personal Strengths

Week 3: Cultivating Gratitude

Week 4: Finding Laughter and Playfulness

Week 5: Fueling Life with Enjoyable and Meaningful Activities

Week 6: Revealing the Springs of Kindness

Week 7: Expanding the Boundaries of Love

Now that we have the map, here are six navigational tips for getting the most out of *A Happier You* and staying on course:

Tip 1: For the program to be effective, try at least some exercises in each practice area, and repeat them several times during the week. You do not need to do *all* the exercises in this book *every* day. Imagine instead that you are choosing from a menu. So, for example, Week 2 offers six exercises around strengths and successes. You might pick four you like—two to repeat during the week and two for the weekends. I encourage you to be creative and flexible with your exercise plan.

Tip 2: Spacing out your use of *A Happier You* can help you learn its techniques more effectively. What might a well-spaced plan look like? Let's look at Week 1. This practice area asks that you work on mindfulness, identify positive feelings, and replay good moments of your day. You might choose to spend ten minutes each morning doing a mindfulness-of-breathing exercise, ten minutes in the afternoon scanning for positive feelings, and ten minutes at night spotlighting your day's best moments. Spreading them out in this way can help if you have a busy schedule. You will also absorb positivity at different points of the day, which can increase how prepared you feel when faced with stressful events.

Tip 3: I suggest you move through the weekly positivity themes in order. While you can skip ahead if you like, the sequence of skills has been thoughtfully planned, with each practice area building on the one that came before it. Of course, you can always spend more than one week on any area, especially if it is working well for you. You can also return to previous areas if you would like more practice before moving forward. *Your* pace is always the right pace.

Tip 4: As with any self-transformation tool, I recommend you use this book with the support of a licensed professional. They can help you tailor it to your unique needs and assist you in getting around obstacles. This is especially true if you live with anxiety, depression, or other serious mental health challenges. *A Happier You* is not a good tool for managing emotional crises. If you are having any thoughts of hurting yourself or others, you should call 911 or go to your nearest emergency room. The bottom line? I want you to be safe!

Tip 5: If your sleep, diet, physical activity, or illness management are suffering, this can make mastering these skills more difficult. Disrupted sleep or a poor diet can drain you of energy and make it hard to focus. Untreated or poorly managed health problems can also draw your focus away from positivity work. This is why professional help with sleep, diet, exercise, or managing chronic health problems may be necessary in addition to the Core Positivity Practices. To benefit most from this book, you might want to seek the services of a registered dietician, sleep specialist, chronic illness expert, or personal trainer, depending on your needs.

How are you feeling so far with this plan? Does it seem doable? I'd like to offer you one last tip.

Tip 6: Don't worry about getting it done all at once. Try to take this journey day by day, week by week. Every step along the way is a form of self-nourishment and you deserve lots of credit for every page you turn. You could think of any time you spend on A *Happier You*, whether it's one minute or twenty minutes, as your "self-care workout." You are building your positivity strength each time you devote any attention to one of these new skills.

Before we begin, I wanted to share a little of my personal history with you. In my life, I have needed, and still need, the skills I am writing about in this book.

Your Happiness Is Within Reach

As a teenager, I struggled quite a bit with depression and anxiety. Although I went to good schools, had friends, earned good grades, played sports, and lived in a warm home where all my basic needs were met, I found myself continually swamped by negative thoughts and feelings. There were times when I could not imagine much of a future for myself, despite the fact that others thought I "had it all."

Fortunately, I received an enormous amount of help from professionals, friends, and family members that enabled me to recover and grow in positive directions. These were the days before positive psychology had emerged as an alternative perspective on change. In looking back, I feel that I would have benefited greatly from a resource that utilized practical ways to improve mood.

As an undergraduate at the University of Pennsylvania, I had an opportunity to learn under Martin Seligman, who is widely recognized as having developed positive psychology and is a leading voice in the field. My interest in this subject continued to grow.

Once I became a psychologist, I had a chance to develop a group program that combined many different positive psychology approaches to well-being. A self-guided version of this program seemed like an important next step. I wanted to create the kind of book that could help people during tough times as well as enhance their lives even when nothing was particularly wrong.

If you are searching for extra support in feeling good or know someone else who is, I hope that this book serves as that guiding light. I continue to practice A Happier You skills in my own life, on good days and bad. I hope you find these skills helpful as you embark on your own journey toward your best possible self.

—Scott Glassman, PsyD

August 2021

The Meadow and the Stream
Catching Positive Events

In all things of nature there is something of the marvelous.   —Aristotle

The well-known expression "I can't see the forest for the trees" captures what it feels like to be flooded by negative thoughts, painful emotions, and deflating events. Walking through this forest of negativity, as many of us do each day, it can be difficult to find a more balanced perspective. It may seem that we are naturally inclined to see the glass as half-empty, resigned to remain lost in that forest, or are unprepared to find a way out. You could blame yourself for being a negative person, but in doing so you would be overlooking a powerful phenomenon that influences all of us, known as the *negativity effect*.

The negativity effect, or negativity bias, describes how something negative can affect you more than something positive, assuming both things have the same intensity. For example, we tend to consider negative information more seriously when forming judgments about people, despite the availability of positive information (Nohlen, van Harreveld, and Cunningham 2019). People spend longer amounts of time looking at negative photographs than positive ones (Veerapa et al 2020). Bad news sells more newspapers and draws more TV viewers than feel-good stories (Trussler and Soroka 2014).

The evolutionary explanation for this effect says that it may be an inherited self-defense reflex. We try to protect ourselves from threats to our survival by paying close attention to what goes wrong.

While this all may sound rather depressing, it's actually helpful when trying to become a more positive and resilient person. Just knowing about the negativity effect can help you step back when caught up in someone else's complaining, when bombarded by news of disheartening world events, or when submerged in your own ruminative thoughts. It also speaks to the importance of having patience with yourself as you begin to stretch new muscles.

Some people may feel the negativity effect more strongly than others. Getting a sense of your "negativity tilt" could help prepare you for this journey out of the forest.

EXERCISE: Measuring Your Negativity Tilt

In this exercise, you will watch your thoughts for a short time as they naturally pass through your mind and see whether you are tilting in a negative or positive direction. Your goal is to become more aware of your thoughts, not to change them. Ready to try? If so, grab a sheet of paper or use the notes app on your phone, and set a timer for two minutes.

Step 1: As your thoughts arise during these two minutes, keep track of whether they are positive or negative. Examples of negative thoughts include, *I wasted the day*, or *I can't see how things are going to get better*, or *I didn't get a call back from my friend. How disrespectful*. Positive thoughts might be, *Tomorrow will be better*, or *I got to at least one thing on my to-do list today*, or *I am still a good friend*. Every negative thought you detect during those two minutes should receive a "-" sign, while any positive thought gets a "+". If a thought seems neither positive or negative, such as *I wonder what I'll have for dinner*, give it an "n" for neutral.

Step 2: At the end of the two minutes, count up how many "+" and "-" signs you recorded. Ignore the neutral thoughts. If you have lots of thoughts that appear during that time, or just a handful, it's all fine.

Step 3: Repeat Steps 1 and 2 three times during the day, or on different days, to account for different events and moods. Record your "+" and "-" totals for each two-minute period.

Step 4: Now add together your "-" thoughts across *all three* sessions. So, for example, you might have three negative thoughts in the first session, two negative thoughts in the second, and four negative thoughts in the third, for a grand total of nine negative thoughts. Do the same thing for your "+" thoughts. Now take a look at your "+" and "-" totals side by side. What do you notice?

Usually, a mix of positive and negative thoughts flow through our minds, but sometimes we tilt one way or the other. The difference may not be very large—for instance, nine negative thoughts compared to five positive ones. On the other hand, you may observe a much stronger tilt toward the negative, such as ten negatives for each positive.

If you believe that negativity regularly dominates your waking awareness, this exercise may reassure you that positive thoughts do indeed cross your mind. But because of the negativity effect, these positive thoughts may go unnoticed, leading you to assume they are less frequent than they actually are, or don't exist at all. The good news is that they *are* present, even if infrequent. Noticing them as they pass by gives you a chance to catch them and put them in the spotlight, a skill we'll be working on soon.

If your positive thinking equaled or outweighed your negative thinking, your positivity tilt is something you can immediately build on. On the other hand, if you watched a lot of negative thoughts pass through your mind during this exercise, you are certainly not alone. Many of us criticize ourselves just for having negative thoughts. This self-criticism, as you might imagine, can produce even more negative feelings. One skill we'll be working on together as we move forward is watching our negative thoughts and feelings without judgment.

The negativity tilt exercise is all about building a greater awareness of what is happening in your mind. No matter what signs you marked down, you have successfully awoken your inner observer. How about we nurture that observer a bit more? Finding the "meadow"—a space in which you can peacefully watch what's taking place, both outside and inside you—will help you do that.

Finding the Meadow

Watching your negative thoughts instead of *being* those thoughts creates a clearing in the forest of negativity. It opens a meadow, a space that allows you to watch what's happening without judgment. When you enter the meadow, you unwrap yourself from the tangle of worries and upsetting feelings about stressful situations in your life. You stand at a distance from them.

The worry and upset are still there, for sure, but as an observer they may not affect you as much. You may even have the feeling of hovering safely over those thoughts and feelings. This is the power of the meadow.

Understandably, you might be wondering, how do I become that observer, other than by counting upsetting thoughts? One way is to use what I call "distancing thoughts." A distancing thought is an observation you make about what's happening inside you.

When I was injured in a car accident many years ago and struggling with severe back pain, one of my most negative thoughts was, *I'll never be the same again.* My first distancing observation was, *I am having this thought right now. The thought is, "I will never be the same again."* Next, I told myself, *This is only a thought. One among many. I am having it because I am in pain. A thought cannot determine my future.*

This distancing self-talk took the sting out of the original thought. I still had the thought, but now I could look at it from afar, safely, without feeling as sad about it. I had stepped into the meadow.

You can try out a distancing approach now, if you like, in this brief exercise:

- Wait for a stressful thought to cross your mind. If you notice yourself feeling sad, anxious, or angry, that may be a sign that one is present.

- Write down the thought. Start with: "The stressful thought I just had was..."

- Now write down your distancing statement, something like "I will allow this thought to go by" or "It happens to be a cloudy day in my mind, and this is one of the clouds."

What did you notice when you distanced yourself from the thought? Did the negative feelings soften at all, or pass more quickly?

If the answer is no, don't be disheartened. I hope you'll see that any effort to step into the meadow deserves praise.

Watching your thinking and distancing both take some getting used to, and it is normal to slip back into the forest as you try. See if you can call forth a gentle, compassionate mindset. Maybe you think to yourself, *Hey, it's normal to get caught up in negativity. I'm learning,* or *It's okay to be a beginner.* If you get stuck back in the forest, you can try to reenter the meadow by saying to yourself, *Let me just watch my difficult thoughts for a while and see what happens.*

Once you find your meadow, you may want to practice staying there for longer periods of time. Watching your thoughts strengthens your observer self. Because you have created a safe space, you can gradually begin to invite more pleasant experiences into it: positive thoughts, feelings, images, memories, hopes, intentions, and actions. Your clearing may at first feel small, broken up by clusters of those dark "thought" trees. But that's to be expected.

As you try out being an observer, you will likely become more mindful. Mindfulness is the practice of stepping out of the stream of daily life and watching with curiosity where it carries you. Mindfulness immerses you in the present moment, which can quiet distress about the past and lessen worry about the future.

Many excellent books focus on cultivating a mindful approach to life. Jon Kabat-Zinn's (2013) *Full Catastrophe Living* and (1994) *Wherever You Go, There You Are* can guide you more fully in developing this skill. For our purposes, mindfulness is not a final goal, but a first step in learning how to bring the best of life and the best of yourself consistently into focus.

Watching upsetting thoughts from a distance highlights another important mindfulness quality: acceptance of whatever it is you happen to observe. You're not fighting with what you discover in your meadow; you're allowing it to be there. Acceptance goes hand in hand with curiosity. It is the essence of self-compassion, which is an important part of the groundwork for positive living.

The Positivity Paradox

It may seem counterintuitive, in a book about creating more happiness and positivity, to practice *not* striving for what feels good. There will be plenty of time later on to work on the intentional creation of positive experiences. But at this early point in our journey, let's watch for the urge to immediately fix, solve, or squash stress and negative feelings. It makes sense that this urge exists, especially if you have a long history of struggling with depression or anxiety.

The problem is that this pressing need to feel better can actually lead to impatience, making pleasant states more difficult to achieve. I call this the Positivity Paradox. The more we push ourselves to change for the better, the more tension we generate. This can cause an emotional backlash in which we encounter *more* negative thoughts and feelings, rather than less.

Imagine that you just broke up with your partner of ten years. How would you feel if you were to tell yourself, *Hey, let it go. Find your "happier you" already. What's the matter with you?* Chances are you would feel more down, frustrated, or self-critical. This demand for positivity comes across as unrealistic and insensitive. It also sends the message that your reaction to a stressful life event is not okay.

The Positivity Paradox also explains why casual advice from others to smile or be happy often falls flat. When others tell you to shake off a bad event, you might think *Easy for them to say,* or *They don't accept me for who I am.* These reactions make a lot of sense. We are not happiness robots that can feel good at the push of a button.

Now imagine a more accepting stance. For the relationship breakup, you might tell yourself, *This is a painful loss. Take whatever time you need to process it.* For daily problems that unexpectedly pop up, you might think, *I can see how upsetting this problem is for me. It makes sense. I can work on solving it and see if the feeling begins to ease.*

These gentle messages might actually help you bounce back faster. When we accept negative thoughts and feelings, they tend to pass more quickly—our next steps often become clearer as a result.

Deep self-acceptance is not always easy to achieve, and of course it is okay to want very much to feel better. You might practice observing that strong desire to feel good. You might think, *In this moment, I am noticing that I feel annoyed with my sadness.* This is a way of embracing your own experience, whatever it is, while keeping the door open to feeling better.

You could also tell yourself, *It's okay to feel this, because it's already here.* This was one of my favorite mindfulness instructions from my training with Steven Hickman, the founding director of the UC San Diego Center for Mindfulness, and with Zindel Segal, coauthor of *Mindfulness-Based Cognitive Therapy.* Whenever I heard this instruction, I noticed the physical tension in my stomach and shoulders diminish. It gave me permission to stop fighting the stress.

Getting in touch with acceptance is like putting out a "Welcome" mat. You plan to meet whatever walks through your emotional door with curiosity and kindness. This does take practice, so I recommend looking for opportunities to do so, by watching the stream of your breath, thoughts, or feelings.

How does all this sound so far? Remember, you can pause any time in this book to repeat an exercise or give yourself extra time to digest what you've read.

Here are two tips to sidestep the Positivity Paradox as you work on acceptance and self-compassion:

Tip 1: During this week, note any time when your self-talk becomes demanding around a goal. It could have something to do with work, family, friends, or another area of your life. For example, you may feel pressure to be more productive at your job or to reach out more often to a family member or friend. You might hear it from within: *Stop moping around,* or *Why don't you keep things neater?* See if you can meet that voice with understanding and acceptance.

Your response could sound something like: *The way things are now does not feel good at all. In this moment, though, I'm going to allow this to be what it is. I trust a better feeling will come, or that an answer to this difficulty will make itself known. I will strive to be patient and work on what I can.*

Please feel free to create your own response, of course. Once you have one that feels true to your inner voice, you could put it in the notes section on your phone, or write it on a note card so it becomes a visual reminder. Sometimes just knowing that you have a supportive answer ready is enough to spur self-compassion.

Tip 2: Another way to sidestep the Positivity Paradox is to remember the flower philosophy, the idea that we have a natural tendency to flourish under the right conditions. This can promote a stronger sense of trust in yourself. It can also remind you that a "feeling good wisdom" already resides within you. Just as you cannot hurry the ways in which a seed absorbs sunlight and water to grow into a flower, you can have faith in the knowledge that you will bloom at your own pace, in your own time.

The Walls Around the Meadow

So far, moving from the forest of negativity into the meadow, a space better suited for establishing your positivity "home," has asked four things of you:

- Greater awareness of the balance between positive and negative thoughts (negativity tilt)

- Observing what is happening within you and around you (distancing)

- Removing the pressure you might put on yourself to feel good immediately (Positivity Paradox)

- Trusting your natural tendency to grow in positive directions (Flower Philosophy of Change)

Sometimes as you embark on a journey like this, you will discover walls around the meadow, blocking entry. The walls you might encounter can include work or family demands, chronic relationship or health problems, a history of trauma, long-term struggles with depression or anxiety, a substance use challenge, or ambivalence about wanting to feel better.

For many, opening the door to positive thoughts and feelings can feel frightening, especially if it represents a brand-new way of being in the world. You may worry about losing support if people begin to see you differently. You may fear disappointment, not making the progress you expected. If you don't consistently feel good, you might be concerned about what that means about you or your future. You may even think that you don't deserve to feel good.

What all of these possible obstacles have in common is some assumption or belief that fuels them. Some examples are, *People won't like the happier me*, or *I'll never be a positive person*, or *I don't have what it takes to change*. After battling depression for years, you might assume, *I am my depression.* You may view yourself as a pessimist, which drains your desire to look for the good in life.

In the spirit of deep acceptance that underlies A Happier You, I invite you to take some time to simply note what your specific walls are and one underlying assumption for each.

It is not always necessary for you to knock down these walls or change anything about these obstacles. Sometimes simply naming the wall or assumption takes away its power. You might, however, have an immediate wall-busting response, like, *Of course I'm not my depression!* or *People must like me, because they call just to talk.*

Here are four other questions you could ask yourself to begin breaking through your walls:

- Which is the strongest wall around my meadow?

- What assumption supports it? Is there any evidence for it?

- If I did not want this wall to stand in the way, what might I do?

- What's one way to bring acceptance to it?

In addition to increasing self-awareness, these questions can strengthen your observer self.

Ready now to take another step forward? The next skill you'll focus on is called *streaming,* a technique that will set the stage for deeper explorations of positive experiences and positive aspects of yourself.

Streaming

Sensations, thoughts, feelings, and images make up your stream of experience. This stream changes from one moment to the next and can take on positive, negative, or neutral tones. You can think of it as a single stream containing all the parts of your awareness, or many streams flowing beside each other: seeing, hearing, feeling, thinking, and remembering.

We first want to practice tuning into this flowing "water" of life. You already started this work by watching negative and positive thoughts. Now I invite you to become the observer again, as you focus on the stream of breathing. Breathing is an always-present motion within you, a continuous flow directly connected to the source of life itself. This makes it a good stream to watch, since its movements are so vivid.

You can either listen to the "Stream of Breathing" audio recording that comes with this book, or read the exercise below, stopping afterward to give yourself time to practice. You can try it with your eyes open or closed, lying down or sitting in a chair, whatever feels most comfortable for you. I recommend setting aside five to fifteen minutes and finding a quiet location where you won't be disturbed.

In the spirit of cultivating self-acceptance, gently note anything that draws your attention away from breathing as you practice. Perhaps say to yourself, *I'm wandering right now, and that's okay.* Then, as best you can, guide yourself back to watching your breath. Don't be concerned if you are pulled away numerous times from your breathing focus. That can be a natural part of the process. Ready to give it a try?

EXERCISE: The Stream of Breathing

If you would prefer to use an audio version of this exercise, visit http://www
.newharbinger.com/47858 to download it.

As you settle into this practice—either standing up, sitting, or lying down, eyes open or closed—just breathe normally. However you are breathing right now is perfectly okay. There is no need to change how fast or deeply you are breathing. Allow your body to breathe as it wishes, at its own pace.

Notice the feeling of air coming into your body and leaving your body. See if you can just watch it flow in and out. Not needing it to be any different from what it is. Being with your body, like a good friend, as it is breathing. Seeing your breath as a stream always flowing through you, always there for you to return to it.

Some breaths may be deeper, some more shallow. Feel your belly rising with each breath in and falling with each breath out. If you notice yourself being drawn away by thoughts or feelings about the future or past, see if you can kindly notice them. You might think, *There's a thought*, or *I am having that feeling*, and then, as best you can, gently bring your attention back to the stream of breathing.

When you are ready to leave the stream, open your eyes if they were closed. Allow movement to slowly return to your hands or feet.

Let's step back and see how that went for you. Are you having any positive or negative thoughts? How does your body feel physically? What emotion is present?

The most important thing to remember is to be gentle and kind toward yourself. It doesn't matter if you were pulled away one time or ten times by thoughts about the past or future. The simple effort of stepping into observer mode means that you are doing it correctly. And, regardless of where your mind goes, you can always come back to the stream of breathing.

Many people say that trying a mindfulness-of-breath activity relaxes them. That is a nice outcome, but not the ultimate goal. In fact, the goal of the Stream of Breathing practice is not to manufacture any particular state of relaxation or to summon positive feelings. In other words, with mindfulness, you are not trying to get anywhere. You simply watch. If the practice left you feeling frustrated, just observing that challenge and how it affects you is itself a success!

Catching Good Moments

Streaming raises your awareness. It allows you to notice all kinds of things—inside and out, good and not-so-good. It is a fine way of becoming less reactive to stressful events and building the skill of accep-tance. If you just watched the stream all the time, however, you would miss the chance to more deeply encounter the moments floating past. This is why we need a net.

With a net, you can scoop out moments from the stream: feeling the warm sun on your face, seeing your child play with friends, or learning about a promotion at work. You can bring these moments closer for careful examination. You turn from watching to catching.

In the stream of life, good things literally dance in front of you, behind you, and above you in the current. But they can be elusive. Just as but-terflies swoop and swirl around us, so do the positive thoughts, feelings, and moments of our day. One might land on your arm, but take flight again before you have a chance to appreciate its beautiful pattern of colors.

You can use a large net to catch a group of positive moments, if you happen to have a stream packed with good things that day. If, on the other hand, you are having a stressful day, you might focus on catching the small, infrequent pleasant events flickering past. You can be very selective about what you choose to examine further. You might not want to take everything out of the net, but only the most beautiful moments, like your child enjoying their playdate.

You may also want to expand the scope of your stream to include not just a day, but the past two weeks of your life. This could increase the likelihood of a catch. You may decide to "catch" for five minutes before returning to watching, or to use the net for much longer. As you net each moment, it may help to jot it down so that it does not slip out and vanish. A word or two will do.

To try out your net, watch the streams of your awareness for a few minutes and see if you can catch a few bright moments. Once they are in your net, decide which one appears most positive and compelling to you.

The Sixteen Signposts

Emotions can help you spot good moments in the fast-moving stream of experience. In this stream, thoughts and images often pass through the mind unnoticed, flying under the radar of awareness. Therapists trained in cognitive behavioral therapy use the term "automatic" to describe these low-fliers.

Feelings, on the other hand, make a bigger splash in the field of awareness—and, as a result, grab your attention more easily. They act as signposts that something worthy of attention is happening, either inside you or around you. A low-flying thought like I won't do well on my performance evaluation at work may give rise to a feeling of anxiety. You may not notice the instigating thought, but you probably feel the lingering effect of the anxiety it provokes: nervousness, tightness in your stomach, and a faster heart rate.

The same thing happens with positive feelings. Have you ever felt happy and not known why? An automatic thought or image probably raced by, leaving an emotional trail of feeling uplifted. When you go back to investigate, you may realize that you were thinking about spending time with a friend. You felt excited about that outing. Connecting a thought with the positive feeling gives you a better understanding of why you felt the way you did. This, in turn, increases your control over feeling good.

For example, you might later decide to think about going out with your friend, as a way of bringing back that feeling of excitement. The faster you can accurately identify the feeling, the more meaning it gives the overall experience and the more control it gives you.

Sometimes we are unaware of both the low-flying thought and its associated feeling, particularly if the feeling has a low intensity. Without a positive emotion vocabulary at your fingertips, catching low-intensity positive experiences from the stream may prove even more challenging. It is always easier to find something when you know what you are looking for.

For all these reasons, we should take some time to expand our awareness of positive feelings. It is helpful to divide them into two categories: active and restful positive emotions.

Positive Emotions

Active positive emotions jump-start your engine. They launch you into activity. Examples include excitement, determination, joy, and inspiration. Spending a day at an amusement park or writing a song could produce this type of emotion. *Restful positive emotions*, on the other hand, contribute to a sense of comfort. They include acceptance, gratitude, and serenity. Taking a warm bath or curling up with a good book come to mind.

Both types of emotions are essential to your well-being. They act as signposts by signaling you to explore the positive moments that gave rise to them. Look at the list below and see if you can pick out some you felt in the past week or two.

Sixteen Positive Emotion Signposts

Active Emotions

- **Excitement:** A feeling of great eagerness and arousing energy

- **Enthusiasm:** Being interested in an active way in something

- **Inspiration:** Feeling highly stimulated to do or create something

- **Joy:** An intense feeling of pleasure, happiness, delight, or elation

- **Love:** A powerful feeling of deep affection, which can be all-encompassing

- **Determination:** A firmness of purpose or commitment to achieving a goal

- **Amusement:** The state or experience of finding something funny or being playful

- **Hope:** A feeling that good things can happen when looking toward the future

Restful Emotions

- **Gratitude:** Feeling thankful about something; ready to show appreciation for kindness

- **Contentment:** A state of satisfaction, or being at peace with what is happening

- **Awe:** A feeling of reverential respect for someone, something, or an event

- **Connectedness:** A feeling of belonging or closeness with others

- **Curiosity:** A strong desire to know, learn, or discover something

- **Pride:** A feeling of pleasure or satisfaction that comes from achievements

- **Serenity:** The state of being calm, peaceful, and untroubled; a feeling of tranquility

- **Transcendence:** Feeling connected with something greater than yourself

If you become familiar with this positive emotion guide, your streaming should result in more catches. The signposts will call out to you! You can look within yourself for any of these sixteen signposts and use them as reminders to pay attention to what is happening alongside that emotion—it could be a thought, conversation, memory, image, belief, expectation, or life event. This next exercise will give you practice in locating pockets of positivity in your life.

EXERCISE: Scanning for Signposts

Scanning for positive emotion signposts is a brief version of streaming, usually lasting no more than a few seconds. To start, you simply drop into your experience at any point throughout the day and see whether one or more of the sixteen positive emotions is present. A launch point question is, "Am I feeling good in any way in this moment?"

You could focus that question on physical sensations, which may be more available in awareness: "Am I feeling good in any way in my body right now?" In doing so, you may discover pleasant sensations, like the sun on your neck or the motion of walking, that lead you to identify the signpost of contentment.

Before you begin your drop-in, you may want to read through the signposts so they are fresh in your mind. If you are doing this on the go, you could carry a small notebook with the signposts written down. A notebook gives you extra possibilities. In addition to having a list easily accessible, you can jot down any positive emotion you catch. You could label whether the feeling is active or restful, and/or rate how strong that feeling is on a 1 to 10 scale.

How about taking a moment to drop in right now? Closing your eyes can make it easier to spot, name, and stay with your positive feelings.

A good goal would be to drop in three times a day (but remember that even one drop-in is a success!). If you don't catch any positive emotions, this is the time for your compassionate voice. See if you can tell yourself, *Nothing here today. But maybe tomorrow there will be.*

As you look for signposts, you also may want to experiment with the "width" of your stream. You could start with a narrow one, say the past ten minutes or so. Or you could choose a very broad stream, looking back across a series of weeks for positive emotional crests.

You may find it difficult to immediately see one of the sixteen signposts when streaming. In that case, it can help if you first bring to mind a positive event, such as a place you went or time you spent with someone. Once you have the event in mind, search that memory for its positive emotional peaks.

For example, you might initially remember going out to eat with a friend, the day you went, and where you ate. Then, as you explore the memory further, you recall that both of you broke into hysterical laughter about something. It is not as important to remember *what* you were laughing about, as it is to recall the *feeling* of laughing that hard with someone you care about. In this example, the signposts of love, amusement, and connectedness may all be present.

How are you feeling with everything we have covered so far? This may feel like a lot to absorb, so I want you to move as slowly as you need. If you would like to stop for a breather or step into the meadow of acceptance, that's absolutely fine! A *Happier You* will be there for you whenever you want to come back to it.

Next, we will look at how to expand the good experiences that surround your positive emotion signposts. This is called *spotlighting*. Before we get there, let's briefly review the three steps in this process:

Step 1: Streaming—Review all the events of a day, the past couple days, or those unfolding right now in the present.

Step 2: Catching—Identify something positive in the stream, or look for a positive emotion signpost and name it.

Step 3: Spotlighting—Bring that positive moment or moments forward for a closer look.

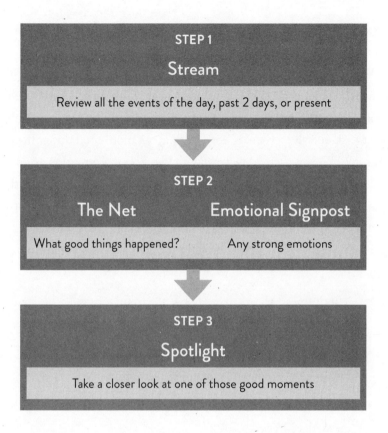

Spotlighting

Mindfulness practice magnifies the moments you catch in your net. People often report that when they place their attention fully on a single object of awareness, it comes alive in ways they had never felt before.

Shining the spotlight of your attention on the leaves of a tree, for example, may cause their color to appear more vibrant. Closing your eyes to focus on a symphony may result in each note sounding brighter. You may suddenly hear separation between the instruments, leading to a richer appreciation of the music. Eating a strawberry mindfully can bring out a fuller range of its flavor and texture. Taking a moment to notice a rose as you are rushing somewhere can fill you with an incredible sense of beauty and awe.

Mindfulness practice can deepen the impact of something good across all of your senses. It can usher in positive thoughts, ignite feelings of enjoyment, and bring up meaningful memories. The question we might want to ask ourselves, then, is not, "Why aren't more good things happening to me?" but rather, "Am I paying close enough attention to all the good things that are happening?" You can rest your attention on anything positive that crosses your path. The more you do, the less the negativity effect will be able to draw your attention to what is going wrong.

Here are three key points about mindfulness and spotlighting good moments:

- Mindfulness allows you to be a careful observer of your life streams.

- When you can catch bright moments from those streams and bring them closer, you can enjoy them more.

- The more senses you use, the more powerful these positive moments can be.

In A Happier You, we want to fill our nets as much as possible with positive events, those that occur inside and out. Through spotlighting, we can maximize the intensity of these good moments by appreciating them in the finest detail possible. "Zooming in" on the good things, no matter how small, is the fundamental skill in this Core Positivity Practice. This next practice, a loosely adapted version of Segal, Williams, and Teasdale's (2013) "Raisin Exercise," will help you start.

EXERCISE: Treating Yourself

This exercise will help you zoom in on the experience of eating something you enjoy. The goal is to slow down your usual process of eating this treat, so that you can experience the full effect of it across four of your senses: sight, touch, smell, and taste. This will show you how to expand other positive experiences in a similar way. You will want to set aside at least a few minutes in a quiet space. If you prefer to listen to this exercise rather than reading it, you can download the audio recording at http://www.newharbinger.com/47858.

First, find something small that you like to eat. It could be a single grape, piece of chocolate, or something else you enjoy. On a scale of 1 to 10, rate how much you usually enjoy eating this treat or snack. Now follow each of the following five steps in order:

Step 1: See and Touch—First, hold your treat in the palm of your hand. Feel its texture. Is it soft or hard, smooth or rough? Notice how the light hits it. What is its color like?

Step 2: Smell—Bring the treat up to your nose and hold it there for a few moments. What does it smell like? Sweet or sour? Does the smell remind you of anything good? As you smell it, are you salivating? Do you notice any anticipatory excitement in your stomach?

Step 3: Taste—Now place the treat in your mouth and close your eyes, but before biting into it, notice its texture on your tongue. Slowly bite down on it and feel how its texture changes. What flavor comes through that wasn't coming through before?

Step 4: Bring the Experience Fully into Self—Chew the treat slowly, and when you swallow it, see if you can track the treat as it moves down into your stomach. With your eyes still closed, think about how this wonderful treat or snack, with all the enjoyment it just gave you across all of your senses, has become part of yourself. See if you can allow that pleasure to linger as long as possible.

Step 5: Rate and Contemplate—The last step in spotlighting is to rate how much enjoyment you experienced by eating your treat in this way, on the same 1 to 10 scale as before.

Let's take a couple minutes to explore what that was like for you. In what ways did eating your treat in this way enhance your enjoyment? Was there a particular sense that stood out? In what ways was this different from how you usually eat something? Did your before and after enjoyment ratings differ?

If you had trouble keeping your focus on the senses, that's okay! It is quite normal for the mind to wander to other things. Just the fact that you were willing to try to zoom in is a wonderful step. It speaks to your broader intention to open yourself up to hopefulness and joy, and there is great power in that alone.

It's also true that the more you practice, the better you will get. To increase your skill, you could set aside a few minutes each day to zoom in on the sight, sounds, and sensations of something enjoyable.

Remember, there is no way you can fail at this. After each try, you might ask the gentle question: "What did I learn from that?"

The Deep Dive

If you tried the spotlighting exercise with a treat or snack, you likely discovered how mindful attention can reveal hidden pleasures in the ordinary experience of eating. What's wonderful is that you can spotlight positive aspects of *any* moment or event in your life. The sixteen signposts can show you where to focus that intense beam of attention.

As with eating the treat, there are spotlight questions you can ask yourself to deepen the encounter and create richer meanings. Here are eight questions to choose from, but feel free to develop your own.

Deep-Dive Questions

- What feels best about this? And why?

- In what ways do my senses come alive through this moment?

- What does this positive event mean about me and my life?

- What other good feelings or positive moments are connected to this one?

- How might this event or moment affect the rest of my day or week?

- What did I do to create such a good feeling? Could I do it again?

- Did the intensity of my signpost feelings increase? If so, how much? And why?

- Who else does this event or moment affect in a good way?

Using one or more of these questions, you can expand moments to reveal aspects of your best self. A seemingly small event, when placed under the spotlight, could speak to your social strengths, spirituality, values, aspirations, milestones, accomplishments, and physical health. For example, hearing birdsong on a walk may represent both good self-care and your transcendent connection to nature. Getting a phone call from a good friend could convey how likable and cared for you are. Something as small as wrapping yourself in a blanket on a cold day could put you in touch with gratitude for shelter and warmth. In this way, spotlighting touches on a wider view of life.

Janessa, a skilled Happier You trainer, used her spotlight during a hike in the mountains with her best friend. She started by watching a series of moments unfold: noticing light breaking through the trees, hearing sounds of birds and a nearby river, and feeling the warmth of her friend's company. When she looked for the signposts, they appeared fairly quickly: contentment, connectedness, curiosity, gratitude, and serenity.

Then, to dive deeper, she asked herself the first question: "What feels best about this?"

This drew her attention more fully to the peacefulness of nature, taking a break from bustling life, and enjoying the connection of friendship. She also noticed that her mind had grown quieter. This quiet space accompanied a deepening sense of physical calm. Janessa had an especially hopeful thought at that point—she could return to this positive space in the future and use it to create other good feelings and thoughts.

She then asked herself the next question: "Why am I feeling thankful for this?"

In response, Janessa felt an even stronger appreciation for the closeness of her friendship. She thought about how her friend had always been there for her, through every major milestone in her life. Together with a heightened awareness of her love of nature, she was reminded that "So much of what I have is what I need."

Spotlighting helped Janessa capture and expand not only immediate pleasures (peace, relaxation, and freedom), but also broader life meanings (friendship, deep caring, and joining with the transcendent side of nature). It also kept stressful thoughts about her many roles and responsibilities at bay, preserving the strength of her positive experience during the hike.

Watching for Positive Thoughts

Another way of using your spotlight involves identifying a positive emotion signpost and then simply waiting for positive thoughts to rise into your awareness around that feeling. When these positive thoughts do emerge, you could ask, "What other good things does that mean for me?"

For example, imagine you are sitting on a sofa, relaxing after a long day of hard work outdoors. You first may recognize a feeling of pride in what you accomplished. Focusing on the feeling could lead to thoughts like *It was great to see the project finished!* and *I did an amazing job* and *People will enjoy that outdoor area more because of my work.* Then, asking yourself what other good things that might mean for you could lead to conclusions such as *I am capable and strong* and *I bring others joy.*

Know that your mind may wander away easily as you watch your positive thoughts. If that happens, remember the instruction in the Stream of Breathing practice: gently, as best you can, bring your attention back to the good feeling, thought, or sensation.

The truth is that negative thoughts can intrude at any time, so this kind of self-redirection may serve you well. It is also good to practice, because positive and negative experiences often get tangled up in each other.

Ultimately, you could experiment with both methods, watching your thinking and asking yourself deep-dive questions, and see which works best for you. Both can produce a chain reaction of positivity, or what I call the "kindling effect." Let's explore that now.

The Kindling Effect

When spotlighting, you may discover that the answers to your deep-dive questions spark additional positive experiences. Focusing on one positive thought or feeling can ignite a variety of them, as if lighting a small collection of twigs to start a campfire.

In the example above, zooming in on completing an outdoor project led to a feeling of pride in the end result, which sparked more general thoughts about being effective in the world and a feeling of excitement about others enjoying that outdoor space. This example of the kindling effect shows how you can sometimes ignite very different positive areas of life: about yourself, your relationships, or overall hopefulness about the future.

As you feed the fire of positive emotions with your deep-dive questions, you may find yourself feeling more creative and open to new ideas, especially when solving problems. Barbara Fredrickson (2001), who specializes in the study of positive emotions, calls this the "broaden-and-build" theory of feeling good. Positive feelings make us more flexible thinkers, which can help us feel more in control of our lives.

Maya's deep-dive example below offers another view of the kindling effect at work. This may be especially helpful if you're faced with a stressful life circumstance.

Maya's Story: The Excitement of Reconnection

Imagine how you might feel if you had to move to a new city without knowing anyone. This was the situation that Maya, a twenty-three-year-old student, found herself in as she began the first year of graduate school. She worried that her meaningful connections with others would fade away, which is not uncommon when you have to relocate. Holidays can further increase these feelings of disconnection, so Maya chose to focus her streaming and spotlighting work on events in her life leading up to Christmas.

As she searched for a positive emotional signpost among those days, one emerged brightly in her memory: excitement.

It was a Thursday afternoon and Maya was on her way to meet a college friend in Christmas Village, a sprawling collection of pop-up holiday vendors in downtown Philadelphia. She streamed the memory of that afternoon in slow-motion: strolling through the Village with her friend by her side, searching for gifts for their families, enjoying the best falafel and fries she had ever eaten, and catching up with each other since they had graduated. They laughed in a way that seemed to erase the ache of their time apart.

Spotlighting these moments of reconnection brought up another good feeling in Maya: comfort. She described a sense of ease that comes from knowing you have someone in your life who is supportive, even if you don't see them every day. She wrote, "It made me feel like I had nothing to worry about, in terms of whether or not I would get in touch with my old friends again."

The spotlighting process deepened Maya's appreciation of friendship, immersing her in feelings of gratitude. "I have friends who really care about me. Really thinking about that afternoon in Christmas Village made me want to treasure all the other moments moving forward, no matter how small." Perhaps even more important, Maya's streaming and spotlighting led her to feel more confident in her ability to build similar friendships in the days to come.

EXERCISE: Stream, Catch, Spotlight

Now it's time to put these new skills together. This exercise will help you do that. It is brief (only five minutes), and you can either find a quiet place to do it or do it on the go. Trying it once a day would be ideal.

To start, feel free to download the "Stream, Catch, Spotlight" work-sheet from http://www.newharbinger.com/47858.

Step 1: Over a five-minute period, watch life carefully as it unfolds, with your net ready to catch and "remove" positive moments from the stream. You can use positive emotion signposts to indicate good moments to spotlight.

Step 2: Once you have identified a moment or event, try a four-question deep dive: "What feels good here?" "Which of the sixteen signposts is it?" "Why am I having this good feeling?" And finally, "What does this experience mean about me or my life?" You can select different questions from the list provided earlier, or use fewer questions if you would like.

Whatever questions you choose, they should be easy to remember, since the ultimate goal is to make this process automatic. In the beginning, however, you could write the questions in a note on your phone, or on a note card or sticky note.

Step 3: See if you can kindle other positive thoughts and feelings during your deep dive. A good prompt for extending your range of positivity might be: "What *other* good thoughts and feelings do I notice here?" If there are sensations associated with your moment, such as taste, touch, smell, or sound, you could explore them as well.

It's possible that one or more of your five-minute streams doesn't produce any good moments to catch. That's okay and not surprising. A good analogy is fishing. There are some outings where you may not catch anything. Try not to get discouraged! You may just need to cast your net somewhere else, or at a different time of day.

You can also use this exercise at night before you go to bed. But instead of watching life as it unfolds over those five minutes, you would spend five minutes streaming your *entire* day and look for moments to pull out. Steps 2 and 3 would remain the same.

If you want to supercharge this exercise, jot down your caught moments in a small notebook. We call this a "positivity catcher." It's a great way to keep a record of what you catch and spotlight. You can come back to it repeatedly over the week for a positivity boost.

Finding the Lighthouses

Sometimes you may not want to stream an unfolding series of present moments or those that took place recently. Maybe you had a really bad day, or a week full of negative feelings. Perhaps you are struggling with a major life stressor, an unexpected loss, a relationship breakup, or a resurgence of depression. You may just feel more discouraged about life in general. The moods triggered by these negative events can cast long shadows over the past, present, and future.

When confronted by the storms of life, it can help to look for especially bright events, with your net in hand. These "lighthouse" events may contain particularly strong positive emotions, thoughts, images, and actions. They often lead to highly detailed, vivid memories and carry such a powerful positive "charge" that the feelings around them can shine more easily through darker moments.

Examples include a surprise birthday party, the first date with someone you fell in love with, scoring a game-winning goal, a wedding reception, your high school or college graduation day, or receiving an unexpected promotion at work.

This next practice will focus on finding lighthouses in your life. You should pick one that has not taken on any new remorseful meanings. For instance, if you recently lost a job you loved, streaming the lighthouse of the original job offer may increase your sadness. See if you can instead search for lighthouses in areas distant from your stress points. For instance, if work is lowering your mood, perhaps search for relationship lighthouses that could raise it.

Is an event coming to mind? If so, follow this series of steps:

Step 1: Picture that event in as much detail as possible. Stream it in chronological order, slowly, from beginning to end. A photograph, video, audio recording, or other physical item connected to that event may help you in re-creating the stream with vividness.

Step 2: As you watch, begin to look for the positive emotion signposts and any related good thoughts. You can also ask yourself these questions to help you explore:

- What were the strongest two or three positive emotion signposts?

- What was the peak positive moment or moments of that event?

- Who else was part of that event and how did they contribute to the positive effects?

- What did that event mean for me at that time in my life?

- How did I feel about the future at that time?

Step 3: Bring any positive feelings and thoughts from that lighthouse more fully into the present moment. This step can really support your happiness in the here-and-now. Here are some questions that can help you make those connections:

- What does this event mean about me *today*?

- Which positive emotion signpost do I feel *most* strongly, right now, as I remember it?

- What thought or physical reminder can keep me connected to this event?

Let's take a moment to reflect on your efforts. How did this exercise go for you? In Step 3, people tend to find that their lighthouses suggest something very positive about themselves in the here-and-now. A first date with your lifelong partner, for example, may remind you of your lovability. A graduation could represent qualities of determination and signal your hopefulness about the future. Receiving a precious gift from a friend or family member may emphasize your capacity for gratitude.

Here is a powerful example from Christine's lighthouse exploration, which strengthened her hopefulness about the future.

Christine's Story: A New Hope for a Healthier Life

Chronic health problems can cause life to feel like an uphill climb. This had been the reality for Christine, thirty-one, who'd been living with a debilitating gastrointestinal disease for over six years. She describes coping with medical issues her whole life and a resulting pessimism that darkened her outlook. Every time something negative would happen to her, she would see it as "another bad thing."

When searching for a recent lighthouse in her streaming work, Christine spotted a flash of enthusiasm and hope. She had just woken up, after undergoing a surgical procedure for her condition, and heard her doctor say that it was successful. As she spotlighted these post-surgical moments, the recovery journey ahead brightened. She felt a surge of confidence that she would experience "health and happiness while on that road."

Taking time to focus on these moments also evoked feelings of comfort, relief, and gratitude, in addition to positive anticipation for the future. Christine practices lighthouse-spotting more often now, recognizing that it fuels her new determination to not let disease define her life.

EXERCISE: Child's Mind—The Photograph

Like Christine, you will be spending some time this week streaming and spotlighting past events, studying them closely for the hidden gems of positivity.

Visual representations of good events are sometimes more effective than words. With that in mind, look for a picture that best captures one or more of the positive emotion signposts. Make that picture your smartphone wallpaper, carry it in your pocket, or put it in a visible location so that you can look at it often.

What do you notice happening inside when you see it? What thoughts arise? Does it kindle other positive feelings or thoughts about yourself, others, or the future?

See if you can talk to someone about your photo. How does it affect your sense of well-being to describe it to them?

Finally, consider what this photograph means about you and your life going forward.

Positivity Across the Dimensions of Wellness

Resilience, or your ability to successfully recover from difficulties, depends in part on using your wellness resources across multiple domains of life: relationships, physical health, leisure, creativity/knowledge, work, finances, and spirituality.

For example, if you feel good about your relationships and physical health, it may be easier to manage a distressing financial situation. If you have a lot of job success, that can keep you feeling positive when you face health challenges or stress in your relationships.

This is why it is worthwhile to identify the area or areas of life that need positivity fuel. Not only can you then take a more targeted approach to your Core Positivity Practices, but you can also draw from your "happiness reserves" from other life domains.

In this brief practice, you'll start out by spotting areas where you could benefit from more support. Then you'll explore your stronger wellness sources, to build your positivity reserves.

Step 1: Rate your overall happiness over the past month, on a scale of 1 to 10, in each of the following areas: relationships, physical health, leisure, creativity/knowledge, work, finances, and spirituality. These domains come from both the work of Margaret Swarbrick (2006) and the Substance Abuse and Mental Health Services Administration's (2016) eight dimensions of wellness. A rating of five or below indicates a need for nourishment in that dimension.

Step 2: Scan for any positive events that emerge in a lower-rated area. If you find one, stream it in detail! Use your spotlighting questions to expand its effects. Draw out all the positive feelings you can. If you are having trouble catching positive events in that area, you may need to create an action plan. For example, to increase positive experiences in relationships, you may need to reach out by phone to a friend more often. Week 5 takes a closer look at the action-planning process.

Step 3: Now stream areas in which you *already* feel good (ratings of seven or higher). For example, if you are having a lot of success at work, you might pick that area to stream, catch, and spotlight. Once you spotlight what's working well in your life, ask yourself, "How might I carry this positive energy into areas of greater need?" For example, thinking about your work success may lead to more-hopeful thoughts about a relationship loss: *I'm really doing well in my job and people highly value me there. That could help me get through this breakup.*

This week, see if you can match your positivity practices to a self-care domain in need of attention, one that you rated five or below on that ten-point happiness scale. You might notice that focusing your attention on a less-nourished area creates more emotional "breathing room." You might also discover that you can better restore your sense of balance, and keep the negative events in your life in the proper perspective.

Reflection Point

We are coming to the end of the first part of your journey out of the negativity forest. So far, your first four Core Positivity Practices are:

- Finding the meadow by accepting whatever is present

- Watching a stream of experience, past or present, to catch its positive events

- Developing a vocabulary of positive emotions to identify good experiences

- Magnifying and kindling positive feelings with the spotlight technique

One of the secrets of feeling good is celebrating your effort. What's something positive you could say to yourself to acknowledge what it took to come this far?

Take a moment to jot down what went well for you, or what you would consider your successes so far. By reading this book and trying some of these practices, you have opened yourself up to new ideas. You have probably also taken a few leaps of faith, to try new ways of experiencing life. You deserve credit for your persistence!

Take a moment too to feel compassion toward yourself if you have encountered any obstacles along the way. It is quite normal to struggle with these new skills. Even though this is a seven-week program, you can pause at any point and take as much time as you need to work on each set of skills.

Now, here is a list of all the exercises we introduced for this week, which you can choose from to create your practice routine:

- Measuring Your Negativity Tilt

- Stream of Breathing

- Scanning for Signposts

- Treating Yourself

- Stream, Catch, Spotlight

- Child's Mind—The Photograph

The additional practices of distancing, exploring lighthouses, and channeling your new skills through the seven dimensions of wellness can be helpful too. While I recommend trying all the exercises and practices at least once, after your initial rounds of practice you can choose which ones you want to keep applying.

This week, look out for negative assumptions like *I'll never be a positive person, so why try?* If you find one, I suggest you put the thought "on trial," examining evidence why it may *not* be true. Writing down that evidence can make it more powerful and may perhaps remove the barrier altogether.

Finally, if you would like to measure the positive emotional impact of completing this week's exercises, you can rate how hopeful and happy you feel on a ten-point scale *before* and *after* the exercises. For example, before trying "Stream, Catch, Spotlight," you may find that your hope and happiness levels are low—a 2 or 3. Afterward, your rating may have increased to a 6 or 7 from the positive charge the exercise gave you. If you prefer a more hands-on approach, you could always add colorful objects to your happiness bucket after the exercise to show the improvement.

If your levels remain lower than you'd like, I encourage you to keep applying the skill! Habits of negative thinking do not typically change overnight, so you may need to repeat these exercises often—a few times a day or more. I also recommend you meet any ongoing distress or frustration with a spirit of compassion, stepping into that meadow of acceptance we talked about at the beginning of this week. Remember, you can always come back to an exercise later if you need some space.

Let's end on a high note. What is one thing that brightened your life as you read through this chapter? Answering this question shows that you are well on your way to discovering your best possible self.

Climbing Mountains
Exploring Successes and Personal Strengths

If you are faced with a mountain, you have several options. You can climb it and cross to the other side. You can go around it. You can dig under it. You can fly over it. You can blow it up. You can ignore it and pretend it's not there. You can turn around and go back the way you came. Or you can stay on the mountain and make it your home. —Vera Nazarian

Mount Kilimanjaro towers 19,000 feet above sea level in the East African nation of Tanzania, attracting 30,000 climbers a year with its majestic volcanic beauty. Although no one knows for sure, the name "Kilimanjaro" likely comes from the Kiswahili people and means "mountain of greatness." Climbing during the wet season usually requires about a week of fighting through very deep mud, fog, cold drizzle, and snowy conditions at the top. This "Everyman's Everest" is a journey that tests the limits of a person's physical endurance and resolve.

On life's path, each of us confronts challenges that loom over us like Kilimanjaro. They can occur at home, at work, while driving or running errands, during conversations with friends—practically anywhere and at any time. Sometimes a high, dizzying summit suddenly and unexpectedly appears in our path: a divorce, car accident, cancer diagnosis, or pink slip at work. Other times we see the mountain well in advance of our arrival, as with marriage, retirement, the birth of a child, and death, giving us ample opportunity to consider how we will tackle it.

Some challenges seem small and may go unrecognized, such as having to work a late night shift, managing a tense conversation with a loved one, or juggling many different responsibilities. You may not stop to appreciate the energy and thought you put into navigating these rocky inclines. Sometimes the world seems to ask you to follow the Nike motto "Just do it," suggesting you need to tough it out and keep going.

Reservoirs of positive emotion lie dormant in the heights you reach. They are present in the summits you stand on after surmounting obstacles large and small. The sixteen positive emotion signposts atop your Kilimanjaro might include relief, pride, hope, determination, and excitement. Your climbs can hold tremendous positive power, regardless of their length, difficulty, or elevation.

How do you start to bring that positive energy and momentum more fully into your life? The answer is something that many climbers do naturally: make stops along the way and look down to see how far you've come. You want to examine, celebrate, and savor everything it took within you to get to each plateau.

Reaching a Personal Summit

Some Kilimanjaros are purely positive. Receiving a good grade on an exam, finishing a long-term art project, or easily winning a sporting competition come to mind. Others are fraught with pain, or feel overwhelmingly negative as you slog your way up. Trudging miles uphill might describe how it feels battling a chronic illness like Lyme disease, forging a path of sobriety, or recovering from an intense surgery.

In A Happier You, we want to start with the more positive type of Kilimanjaro, the mountains you have scaled that offer easy access to your positivity reserves. In Week 1, you went back in time to identify lighthouses, those bright, memorable occasions in life that are packed with positive thoughts and feelings. In this first exercise of Week 2, I invite you to return to one of the lighthouse events you discovered and look at it as though it's a mountain you've conquered.

You want to stand on the summit and look down, measuring and appreciating *all* your efforts that led up to that experience. This is an important first step in becoming aware of your strengths. I encourage you to study everything that helped you climb to that point: the time, energy, good decisions, self-talk, grit, and sacrifices. Even if your contributions are not immediately apparent, surely there is something you did to help *create* that good place in your life.

Consider a positive self-statement, such as *I honor the work I've done to make this a reality*. A statement like this can inspire you to look for your strengths. You can repeat it silently to yourself whenever you need that extra spark.

Spotlighting the Climb

As you stream your lighthouse event, see if you can identify the positive emotion signposts. Closing your eyes should increase the vividness, detail, and intensity of the stream and bring these signposts to the surface. Feelings of hope and enthusiasm often burn brightly there, illuminating possibilities for growth and success.

As you move through the event stream, try to answer one or more of the following questions, in your mind or on paper. These questions should give you a clearer picture of your "climbing skills" and reveal empowering messages about yourself as an individual and about your life as a whole:

- What positive qualities did I show that helped me get to that place?

- What was the hardest part about getting to the "summit"? How did I tackle it?

- What does that accomplishment mean about me, my specific abilities, and my future?

- Which feelings of purpose and meaning came from that event?

- Was a caring person around me at that time? If so, how were my efforts connected with that relationship?

- What kind of energy and momentum did that accomplishment generate? In what ways did I keep that ball rolling?

- How does bringing that stream into focus now, in the present moment, inspire me?

- When would it help the most to return there in my mind?

As these questions help you recognize your capabilities, you will likely accept and prize yourself at deeper levels. You may feel less vulnerable to the voice of your inner critic. You are also more likely to see yourself as someone who *can* versus someone who *cannot*.

In response to these questions, a new parent might acknowledge being strong enough to ask for advice when needed. Athletes might say they didn't let training setbacks stop them from pursuing their competitive goals. A first-generation college graduate might highlight the unwavering love of family and friends as essential in helping them reach that milestone.

Colleen, a forty-four-year-old working in the real estate industry, was able to see her strengths in having changed jobs within her field. She spotlighted her ability to push through the fear of the unknown around entering a new work environment. In streaming this event, she identified a key thought that made her feel more positive about the transition: *Every new job teaches me strength, offers new learning experiences, and gives me a chance to meet new people.* This encouraging thought, along with her use of music and meditation, contributed to a calming sense of trust and patience as she navigated the job change.

By asking herself the spotlight question, "What does this transition mean about me and my future?" Colleen more clearly saw her ability to tackle life's challenges in general, and to grow from them. She wrote, "No matter what the future holds, I can remain positive about learning new things." She noticed feelings of excitement, determination, gratitude, and hope emerging as she explored the job change at this depth. It revealed wisdom, another strength of hers, as she thought, *Sometimes the doors we close can be a very good thing for us.*

If you still feel doubtful about your abilities and strengths after answering some of these spotlight questions, perhaps give yourself some time to try the exercises ahead in this week and see if that doubt diminishes. If you like, feel free to download the "Spotlighting Strengths" worksheet from http://www.newharbinger.com/47858.

For a number of reasons, many of us grow up with a *cannot* mindset that is tough to break! To begin to change that belief takes patience, self-compassion, and a willingness to continue searching for evidence of strengths. Stepping for a moment into the meadow of acceptance could be especially helpful here.

Making Your Home on the Mountain

As you work with your own positive Kilimanjaro from the past, you'll likely notice some of the sixteen positive emotion signposts filling your awareness. What happens, though, when the stream ends? The visual review of even our brightest memories is time-limited. When the images stop, like a tape ending, the mind's screen may go dark.

You can help keep the feelings alive, however, by continuing to ask yourself questions. You can extend the exploration. For example, after your streaming exercise, you might ask yourself, "Where am I experiencing these signposts most vividly in my body?" or "What other good thoughts or memories are coming up?" You could lengthen the effect through an invitation or quietly expressed intention: *I invite these feelings to remain within me as long as possible* or *I wish to hold these feelings from that time close to my heart.* You might capture an especially powerful thought from the stream and repeat it in your mind. In Colleen's example, reframing her job departure as an opportunity for growth lifted her confidence and mood.

You make your home on the summit of the mountain this way. It is similar to sitting with legs crossed at the overlook point, enjoying the warmth of your accomplishment. The good feelings could linger for a few minutes, an hour, or even longer. What matters is that you are working to extend their stay. Once they do fade, remember that you can always return to this spot to feel that moment's inspiration, hope, and comfort.

Shining Brightly on Dark Climbs

In December of 2005, New York City firefighter, marathon runner, and 9/11 first responder Matt Long was riding his bike four blocks away from his apartment when a bus made an unexpected right-hand turn and struck him (Long 2011). Matt found himself crushed underneath, impaled by the bicycle's seat post, bones broken throughout his body. As EMS workers raced to free him, he lost massive amounts of blood. At the hospital, trauma doctors gave him a 1 percent chance of surviving that first night.

In spite of the grim prognosis, Matt did survive the night, as well as the ones that followed. Given the extent of his injuries, a grueling climb up the darkest of Kilimanjaros had just begun. Matt spent five months in the hospital and underwent forty-two surgeries within the first fourteen months of the accident. One could say that each surgery was its own mountain. He describes falling into a deep depression, at one point writing "Do Not Resuscitate" on a surgery consent form. Matt, who could run a marathon in just over three hours before the accident, could only walk fifty feet on crutches upon leaving the hospital.

A pivotal moment came when Matt's mother showed him some tough love. After that day, Matt started to tell himself that he would be an athlete again, committing himself to reclaiming an essential part of his identity before the accident. He found a functional performance center in

Arizona that welcomed his mission to run again. Three months after moving to Tempe to continue his recovery, Matt ran a mile in eighteen minutes. He eventually ran a marathon in seven hours and twenty-one minutes, but refused to stop there. He became an Ironman again by swimming 2.4 miles, cycling 112 miles, and running a full marathon.

Matt's story teaches us that you can make a comeback from the most dire of circumstances. A natural strength resides in you, regardless of the distance you have to travel and the difficulty of the journey. This strength is present even during periods of profound despair. What's more, the traumatic life events in your path could be opportunities to discover the unshakable foundation of your character.

Small Steps Matter

A journey through darkness does not need to be as difficult as Matt's in order for you to feel a sense of accomplishment. Each step up the dark side of Kilimanjaro asks to be not only recognized, but also celebrated. I encourage you to spotlight and appreciate every sign of that strength, no matter how small or unimpressive the step forward seems, no matter who seems to be running faster than you.

For example, you could decide to focus on your good performance evaluations at work even though others might be receiving promotions. If you have not left your home for days because of depression or anxiety, you could spotlight that first trip outside, even if it's brief; you could choose to honor the courage it took to step out the door. If you just started a long educational journey, you could celebrate every semester you finish, or every completed assignment. There are so many ways in which we grow in life. We want to catch as many as we can.

Like Matt, *your* definition of progress is the only one that matters. He did not seem to mind finishing next to last in a marathon. His brother shouting "I love you!" at the finish line fortified his spirit and filled his heart.

Where you started your journey and where you are today are the most important points of comparison. I encourage you to stop and look back frequently as you climb those tough mountains. Awe is your ally. The voice inside that says, *Wow, look how far I've come already!* can propel you forward, sustaining your momentum through the toughest parts of the ascent.

EXERCISE: Dark Climb, Bright Steps

Think about a dark, difficult climb in your life. It could be something happening now, a recent event, or a tough time as far back as early childhood. Stream it in as much detail as possible, as much as you are comfortable. Some painful memories can be difficult to contain once they are activated, so please be sensitive to your limits and stop the exercise if you begin to feel overwhelmed.

As you stream the climb, guide yourself with these questions:

- How did I meet that challenge? What qualities helped me on my ascent?

- What mile markers of progress do I see in that climb?

- Did those "steps up" seem as bright or meaningful at the time? If not, in what ways do I appreciate them now?

- What do I treasure about the strength or strengths I showed?

- How does thinking about my "bright steps up" help me today?

Some of the sixteen positive emotion signposts may appear when answering these questions. Common ones are determination, hope, enthusiasm, and gratitude. Keep in mind too that tough climbs in life are not always a direct ascent. Climbers often have to move sideways, and even back down, before they can find a clear path to the summit.

Successful recovery from mental illness and addiction, for example, often includes relapses or "steps backward." Instead of seeing them as something to avoid or feel ashamed of, I wonder if you could look at them as learning experiences necessary for your personal growth. Perhaps you could ask yourself, "How did stepping back actually help me move forward?"

Doug's story demonstrates how spotlighting strengths during a painful life event can help us cope in positive and active ways, building our resilience and revealing special meanings that may lie hidden there.

Doug's Story: Caring for a Loved One at the End of Life

A terminal illness is one of the darkest climbs anyone has to make. It can consume a family with sadness and pain, but it can also reveal that family's unique strengths in the ways it comes together. Doug experienced both sides of this difficult journey as his brother began to grapple with end-of-life medical issues.

A giving, energetic, and positive person, Doug leaped into action. To support his family, he moved in with his parents, left his job for two months without compensation, and put his graduate work on hold.

As he streamed the events over those months, a variety of personal strengths emerged in his spotlight. Doug became more aware of his love for his family, how it drove him to drop everything to be there for them. He acknowledged the courage it took to put aside differences so he could be fully present. His strength of gratitude surfaced as well, a thankfulness for the Family and Medical Leave Act, which allowed him to keep his job.

Doug also saw how this experience added to his wisdom about life, highlighting the importance of putting others' needs first and the value of caring for a loved one at the end of life. He appreciated the gift of feeling closer to those who mattered most to him. His search for strengths within the stream also fostered a deep sense of peace and centeredness amid the melancholy of his approaching loss.

When Doug placed his struggle under this supportive spotlight, he found a greater clarity around his values, the meaning in loss, and a stronger connection to others—all of which kept him moving forward.

Making a Mountain Out of a Molehill

During childhood, we come to think of "success" as the sum of our most impressive and visible achievements: scoring a goal in a soccer game, earning a school award for outstanding behavior, being picked first for a team, or receiving exemplary grades. This idea of success as a top-tier "win" follows us into adulthood. It can include wealth, physical fitness, job advancement, abundant friendships, children who excel, or celebrated community roles. It is perfectly fine to want these things in life, to work hard for them, and to feel pride when reaching such high elevations.

At the same time, it's easy to fall short and feel "less than" when the bar of success floats so high over our heads. Perhaps you lose a job, a romantic relationship falls apart, your essay is rejected by a publisher, or your children get into trouble at school. Having such a high bar of success can cause you to ignore the positive parts of life's journey. It can lead you to put all your eggs into the basket of arriving at an impressive outcome. This can drain your appreciation of the enormous effort you put into life, even when you don't get all the way to where you were hoping to go.

You might overlook how you worked hard to save that relationship or job. You might neglect the courage of having submitted something for publication. You might devalue your creative solution to helping your child perform better in school. As you did in the Dark Climb, Bright Steps exercise, you want to spotlight the hidden gems of your effort and problem-solving, even when things don't work out.

To increase our capacity to feel good, it helps to redefine success as any degree of *progress*, *effort*, or *learning*, while moving toward a desired goal. This sets the bar at a much more reasonable height. Each action taken toward something positive can be more fully enjoyed. In this respect, you can succeed each day in small ways in whatever you do, as a parent, coworker, student, or any other role you have in life.

It is quite okay, then, to make a mountain out of a molehill. It is okay to begin prizing ordinary parts of your daily routines, whether that's organizing your closet, driving a long distance to a job, making yourself a nice breakfast, or answering email. Others may not see these things as personal triumphs, but what counts is what *you* see, what *you* feel it took to take that step.

How many good molehills are waiting for you to pay attention to them? This next exercise will help you find out.

EXERCISE: Magnifying Your Molehills

To create your first magnified inventory of successes, it will help if you have your positivity catcher notebook or a notes app on your phone handy. It will also allow you to easily look back at past inventories, in case you want to compare lists from different days. This exercise will probably take about fifteen to twenty minutes, depending on the size of your list.

Step 1: Make a list of things you did today, from the time you woke up until now. Include actions that seem ordinary, like brushing your teeth, taking out the trash, making a meal, or calling someone on the phone. List as many as possible, so you catch everything in the stream. You don't need to list them in the order they occurred.

Step 2: Once you have your list, circle, check off, or highlight items that took the most effort or energy, or were noteworthy for any reason.

Step 3: Ask yourself the following questions about each item you highlighted:

- Was there something challenging about it? If so, what?

- What good came out of it? What were the benefits? (It's okay if you only see one benefit, like feeling satisfied after a meal or refreshed after a bath.)

- How did that action positively affect me, physically, emotionally, or socially?

Step 4: The last part of your spotlighting involves creating a summary statement for each item that begins with "This is a personal success because..." Notice what positive emotion signposts arise as you focus on this last step.

Here are two examples of magnification from a Happier You participant, Greg, which resulted in a stronger sense of well-being and meaning.

Example 1

One action I took today: Dropped off absentee ballot application

What was most notable or important about it? Will enable me to vote during this election year

Benefits: A sense of purpose

This is a personal success because: It reflects my strong belief in contributing to the greater good

Example 2

Another action I took today: Rested in the backyard

What was most notable or important about it? I rarely take time to rest and relax

Benefits: Feeling especially calm

This is a personal success because: I took care of myself

When Greg magnified these actions, he saw more clearly how they resulted in renewed energy, lower stress levels, and a sense of accomplishment. He took much-needed time to recharge and fulfilled a civic duty that could positively shape the future. In his spotlight, Greg saw how these actions also satisfied his values of self-compassion and consideration for others.

After completing the exercise, you might want to rate, on a scale of 1 to 10, your sense of accomplishment to fully appreciate the spotlight's effect. The more you magnify your accomplishments like this on a daily basis, the less likely you are to think, *I didn't do anything worthwhile today.* That, in and of itself, can open the door to positive feelings.

Anthony offers us another example of using magnification, in this case to help reshape a frustrating situation.

Anthony's Story: A Not-So-Small Success of Persistence

It was a Saturday night and Anthony, a thirty-three-year-old financial operations coordinator, felt his irritation growing as he searched unsuccessfully for a specific item his wife had asked him to pick up at the supermarket. He found himself walking up and down the same aisles repeatedly and was seconds away from giving up.

Anthony made a seemingly small decision at this point. He took a deep breath and told himself, Take your time and focus on looking *at the shelves more closely.* Sure enough, he found the item in the first aisle he had looked in.

Streaming that success the next day filled Anthony with feelings of relief, happiness, and pride. He wrote, "Normally, I would have given up quickly or called my wife to tell her I couldn't find it." He identified persistence and self-control as two key strengths that emerged in that moment. Anthony had the thought, As long as I stick to the task at hand, no matter how big or small, good results will come.

What some might consider a small success led Anthony to feel significantly more hopeful about the future. In his deep-dive spotlight, he saw himself as a stronger person, more confident in his ability to overcome obstacles. This fueled his determination to reach his goals in other areas of life, such as becoming a first-time home buyer.

A List of Mountains Conquered

You may not want to take inventory of your strengths *every* day. Quite honestly, sometimes we just need to get through a tough day and wait until the storm has passed to process what happened. A twelve-hour shift of grueling work, a day of toddler misbehavior, or a combination of things going wrong may leave little room for reflection. On days like these, the meadow of acceptance may be a more helpful place to spend your time. Your best self-care option at ten p.m. might be sleep, not a *Happier You* exercise!

Timing really is everything. Sometimes letting some days pass before you go back to look for strengths or practice magnification makes sense. Instead of identifying your steps up the mountain at the end of each day, you could wait until the end of the week. You could set aside some time on a Friday or Saturday for a "Week in Review" session. At that point, you could create a "mountains conquered" list.

On the other hand, you may not want to wait until the end of the week. Maybe you want a self-confidence boost each day. If so, you could schedule a "mountains conquered" midday check-in. Two spotlighting questions that could be helpful here are, "What have I accomplished so far today?" and "How might this affect the rest of my day or week?"

Either way, your "mountains conquered" list could contain:

- All positive accomplishments during the week, as many as you can think of, no matter how small; *or*

- Only major accomplishments, the biggest steps you took.

Once you have your list, spend some time taking it in. See what positive emotions the accomplishments bring out in you. You could pick one or two mountains from the list, stream what happened, and spotlight the effects with questions from Step 3 of the Magnifying Your Molehills exercise.

Here is another question that could help here too:

- How do the smallest mountains I conquered this week move me closer to achieving my larger goals in life?

Be ready for big, sweeping, feel-good answers from this one. For example, completing a résumé could represent a key step toward the career you've always wanted. Reaching out to someone new could be an important step on your way to creating a larger support network. These meanings can then generate *more* positive feelings and thoughts, similar to the kindling effect from Week 1.

As you may have gathered, there is no single right way to take stock of your successes. The right way is what works best for you, and it may take some trial and error (and patience) to discover. Whatever time you need is fine.

The Flower Philosophy Revisited

In the introduction, I talked about how a beautiful blossom already exists within a flower seed, even before it is planted. With the right mixture of soil, sunlight, and rain, the flower's color, scent, and form naturally emerge in their fullest expression. It is also true that flowers and trees grow toward the light. They seek it out, stretching out of the shadows in order to reach it—sideways if necessary. They seem to figure out on their own where the sun falls. Once they do, they show an unflappable determination to get there—an urgency, even.

Similarly, as human beings, we have a natural inclination to grow toward what we desire, striving for the things that give us meaning and joy—the sunlight of life, such as friendships, romantic relationships, fulfilling jobs, and a comfortable home. You could say that we have a built-in intention to climb over the barriers that stand in our way.

The way I see it, merely *sensing* your intention to thrive qualifies as a success, even if you have not yet taken a first step. It reflects the way you're honoring your natural inclination to find your ideal growth conditions.

We also *want* challenges in our lives, since they reveal our strengths, give us purpose, and help us grow. Climbing your personal Kilimanjaro to reach a valued goal is probably preferable to being airlifted to its summit. How would you know your strength if you had no heavy items to lift?

In this way, mastery and accomplishment are key parts of the "good life," as Martin Seligman (2012) has described in his revised understanding of positive psychology. Feeling good depends in large part on feeling capable and effective, and to feel capable and effective we need challenges and obstacles to overcome. It may take some time to believe we have what it takes to endure. Or we may be helped by someone else's perspective, as this next story shows.

My Story: "You Come from Tough Stuff"

I found the letter a year after my father passed away. My mother and I were cleaning out his office when we discovered a sealed envelope with my name on the front.

I opened it slowly as my heart raced, wondering what it might contain. It turned out to be a final message to me, written years earlier, perhaps prompted by my father's fear that his cancer would progress quickly.

In the letter, he shared his thoughts about what mattered most in life, his regrets, his never-ending love for me, and a promise that he would always be present whenever I needed him. One line in particular struck a deep chord; I must have read it three or four times, trying to fully absorb it: "Go forward with the knowledge that you come from tough stuff."

I had always admired my father's strength, resourcefulness, and independence in life. He was the humble son of a furniture-maker who worked hard to become a successful doctor. No problem seemed too big for him; there seemed to be no storm he couldn't weather. Perhaps these qualities were attributable to growing up during World War II. The line in his letter struck me because it conveyed that he always saw the same strength in me, even when I did not. In his eyes, the fortitude was there.

The truth is, we all come from tough stuff. While humanity consists of a softness and fragility, it also possesses an inherent toughness. Every cell in the human body contains some of the same organic compounds that can be found in sedimentary rocks. I find that amazing! Quite literally, strength is woven into the fabric of our beings. To fully appreciate our hardiness, however, we need to hear the music of our unique personal strengths.

The Music of Our Strengths

We tend to think about strengths as the specific things we are good at in life, such as writing, math, playing an instrument, athletics, parenting, organizing, leading a team, listening to others, or any other ability we have worked to develop. But it is also helpful to think of our strengths in an abstract way, as broad personal attributes that contribute to success in many different areas of life. For example, creativity, bravery, and wisdom are all strengths a soccer player might rely on during a game. The same strengths could help with managing complicated life stressors like a divorce.

What strengths, specific or broad, do you know you possess?

If you are hesitant to focus on your strengths for fear of coming across as arrogant, I would like to formally grant you a lifetime "Strengths Exploration Permit." This permit allows you to listen for and celebrate the music of your best qualities. Listening for strengths does not have to be a boastful process; it can remain a private recognition of the special qualities that help you thrive across different situations. And it's okay if others do not "hear" those attributes. What's important is that *you* hear them.

When you quietly notice where you excel, you invite in a joy in who you are, which builds confidence. Outside validation feels good, for sure, but we know we are truly happy when we don't have to prove ourselves to anyone.

You can tune your ear to your strengths in the past, as far back as early childhood. Maybe you were outgoing, creative, or athletic back then. Listen again for a moment. Can you hear any of the same strengths in you today? Maybe new ones have emerged over the years, like being conscientious, organized, or committed to social justice.

Through their research, Christopher Peterson and Martin Seligman (2004) have identified a set of twenty-four strengths, to help us better hear the music of our strengths. I split them into three categories, or octaves (emotional, social, transcendent), and either reworded or combined a couple to make them a little easier to remember.

The Three Octaves of Personal Strengths

- **Emotional:** love, bravery, vitality, humor, gratitude, hope, self-control, integrity, perseverance

- **Social:** leadership, teamwork, social intelligence, fairness, forgiveness, kindness, open-mindedness/acceptance

- **Transcendent:** spirituality, appreciation of beauty and excellence, wisdom, creativity, curiosity/love of learning

Take a few moments to review these categories and circle or write down which strengths best describe you. Completing the VIA Character Strengths Survey at http://viacharacter.org could also guide you in identifying your top strengths. Based on the list above or the survey results, you can choose which strengths fit you currently, or felt more true in the past. Even if they felt like a better fit in the past, remember that these strengths by their nature still reside within you, waiting to be recognized again.

Have a look at what you've circled so far. You can consider this your "strengths profile," a unique combination of personal strengths that contribute to your success and happiness. In the next exercise, you will continue to build that profile by spotting your best attributes in the good things that happen to you.

EXERCISE: Your Symphony of Strengths

I can't think of any songs made from a single note. Like songs or symphonies, our strengths are composed of a variety of notes and chords, played at different volumes and octaves, and at different times.

One day you may hear your emotional octave loudly, noticing strong examples of persistence and vitality. For example, you might have figured out how to fix something after several tries, and later spent time in nature to recharge. On another day, you might hear the quieter notes of spirituality and curiosity. Maybe you prayed in the morning and read a book about your favorite hobby in the afternoon.

You can miss this music if you aren't listening carefully for it. This exercise will help you discover and hear the music of your strengths amid the noise of life. Once you do, you will closely examine each note for its meaning, attempting to keep that meaning with you by letting it linger in your spotlight. As with previous exercises, you will want to find a quiet place where you can remain undisturbed for ten or fifteen minutes. Ready to start listening?

Step 1: Start out by identifying a positive event in your life, past or present.

Step 2: Once you locate something, stream the experience like you did when catching positive events in Week 1, replaying it slowly. Closing your eyes, if that feels comfortable for you, allow yourself to really *feel* any of the sixteen emotion signposts that may rise up. Notice any positive sensations in your body as you replay that event, such as lightness in your belly, less tension in your muscles, or an adrenaline rush if the event was exciting. Welcome any positive thoughts that arise.

Step 3: Now ask yourself, "What strength of mine helped make this experience positive?" If none immediately come to mind, read through the strengths list to see if one or more fit. Does one octave in particular jump out—emotional, social, or transcendent?

Step 4: Finally, to hear the full depth of the note (or notes), ask yourself, "What does showing that strength mean about me or my life going forward?" and "In what ways is it a success?"

With each question you answer in these steps, you give your song greater resonance and depth. Surviving an abusive relationship, for example, may become much more than an act of self-preservation. By the time you reach Step 4, you might see it as a triumph of heightened awareness, self-respect, hope, and resourcefulness. Maybe you spotlighted a decision to go to a party where you didn't know many people. Streaming moments of being funny and talking to different people could uncover additional strengths in your "social octave," such as likability, kindness, and acceptance of others. This exercise may have a lot of encouraging surprises in store, as it did for Silina.

Silina's Story: Sharing Lessons in Life

Silina is an energetic, undeniably positive person who deeply values her bond with others. She brings her best self to work each day and takes great pleasure in a healthy lifestyle, one rooted in a love for yoga.

Late one Tuesday evening, while sitting in her home office, Silina streamed the previous weekend, searching for something good that happened. She settled on the time she spent that Saturday with a group of four young women around her kitchen table. They talked openly for hours about life and how its challenges presented opportunities for change.

Streaming this event brought a rousing symphony of positive qualities into Silina's present-moment awareness: wisdom, open-mindedness, vitality, and leadership. "The feeling of success came from knowing that I made a 'deposit' as the elder of the group," she wrote, referring to her contributions to their personal growth. In recalling what she shared that day, her message of resilience to these women shone the brightest. As part of that message, Silina talked about her hard times as the foundation that she continues to stand on today.

In addition to feeling fulfilled by this unique chance to mentor others, Silina felt courageous and thankful—other notes joining the music of her strengths. She was grateful for the trials in her life that taught her important lessons. She cherished the chance to help these young women at a critical time on their own life journeys.

Like Silina, you can start with a positive event and spotlight your best qualities surrounding that event. You could also start with the strengths themselves and work backward, finding specific examples of that strength in your life and deepening its music by asking questions about the feelings and meanings around those examples.

Deepening the Music

If Silina had started from her strengths and worked backward, she might have first read the list of social strengths and chosen the attribute of leadership to explore. She could have then asked herself, "When is the last time I showed leadership?"

This question most likely would have guided her attention to the Saturday meeting. A follow-up question could have deepened its significance in her life: "In what ways did I lead, and how did these actions affect my thoughts, feelings, and relationships?" The more examples we find of a strength, the more true that strength will feel.

I invite you to try that approach now. You may want to start by reviewing the three octaves of strengths presented earlier: social, emotional, and transcendent. You could choose one strength from each category and look back in time for examples.

Whether you choose to work backward from the strengths lists, or allow strengths to emerge naturally out of positive events, the end result is the same: you are bringing the best *you* to the forefront of your awareness.

You don't have to rely on questions alone to deepen the music of your strengths. You can do it through the senses as well. This next exercise will show you how.

EXERCISE: Child's Mind—The Rock

Sometimes we want more vivid and immediate contact with our strengths, as opposed to merely thinking about them. Our senses can help us. Sight and touch, in particular, have the ability to directly connect us with our best attributes.

To start out, find a small stone, rock, gem, or some other portable object that is hard to break, preferably something from the natural world. Your stone, rock, or other object will represent one of your personal strengths (love, social intelligence, wisdom, etc.). This week, whenever you see or touch this rock or object, visualize that strength filling your body and heart. Allow examples of it to enter your mind. The weight and density of the rock or object should remind you of your chosen strength's solid presence within you. Notice the good feelings that this connection brings out.

Try to keep the rock or object with you, so that you have many opportunities to sense its meanings throughout the day. A pocket is a great place for it! You can literally take this strength with you wherever you go. It can become a part of whatever you do. You can also assign it a different strength each day, observing how your contact with it affects the quality of your emotional, social, and physical well-being.

If working backward from a strengths lists, or carrying an object to represent your strengths, doesn't deepen your appreciation for your best qualities in the way you'd like, you might want to turn to others for their perspective. Strengths interviewing is a social way of bringing out your best possible self.

Strengths Interviewing

Sometimes a difficult childhood, depression, anxiety, or chronic worry can hide the music of your strengths. A bad day or week can do the same thing. If you have trouble feeling connected to any of the strengths listed earlier, you can always turn to others and ask them what they see.

If you can, find a safe person to be your partner, someone you trust and feel close to. Once you've found a quiet place and a time when neither of you are in a rush or preoccupied, ask this person to identify your best qualities. Do the same in return for them.

Next, take turns diving deep, as you would in a spotlighting exercise. Ask your partner for examples of those qualities and reciprocate by offering some examples related to your partner's strengths.

Finally, observe and share what positive feelings arise in the conversation. You might even want to look at the positive emotion signpost list as a point of reference.

Don't be surprised if you feel even closer to your partner after this practice. On the other hand, if talking like this feels awkward, you could exchange "strengths notes" instead. You could write a strength you notice in them on a sticky note and leave it someplace they are likely to discover it, like the inside of a drawer or cabinet they often use. They could do the same for you. You could schedule a week of these exchanges.

In addition to learning about your best qualities through another's point of view, you can plan time to get in touch with specific strengths this week. Let's explore what that would look like.

A Get-Together with Your Strengths

Sometimes our strengths may be "sleepy," meaning they are not active or easily seen in our lives. It may be harder to find them in the course of our daily routines, especially on stressful days.

If this is the case, look back at the lists of personal strengths in each of the octaves and circle a couple you would like to "get together with" in the week ahead. Then make a tentative plan to bring out that strength.

For example, if you selected teamwork, see if you can collaborate with a coworker on a project in the days ahead. If your strength is spirituality, you could schedule time to pray or connect in some way with your higher power.

In these get-togethers, you are creating examples of strengths, which you could later spotlight at the end of the day in your positivity catcher notebook. After you have "woken up" a strength in some way, you can also rate how happy, optimistic, and in control of your mood you feel, on a scale of 1 to 10. Alternatively, you could add more colored objects to your happiness bucket to better visualize how the level has changed. Either way, stepping back like this and asking, "How am I different now?"

will give you a better idea of what your best fit is for the activity you choose.

Remember that your planned get-togethers should be flexible. Let's say your plan to collaborate with a coworker falls through, but you still want to bring out a strength related to your job. You could then choose a different strength in your social octave, such as leadership, by proposing a new project or taking the lead on an assignment. You could also move to an entirely different octave in a different life domain, like the emotional strength of love within your family, looking for opportunities to laugh and feel grateful with them. When you consider the many sides of wellness, there really are so many possible strength combinations. That's what we're going to explore further now.

EXERCISE: Successes and Strengths Across Wellness Dimensions

One of the options for Week 1 involved identifying positive events in one or two wellness areas in need of a boost: relationships, physical health, leisure, creativity/knowledge, work, finances, or spirituality. This exercise asks that you search for evidence of accomplishments and strengths *across* these areas. In this way, you are casting a wider net, looking at positives in as many self-care areas as possible. A good time to cast your wellness net would be at the end of the week.

> **Step 1:** On a sheet of paper, create sections corresponding to each wellness domain, leaving plenty of space for notes within these sections.

> **Step 2:** Take a look at the list of strengths from earlier and then ask yourself, "What wellness areas of my life did I show a strength in this week?" Place any strength you spot in its related column. If you forgave a friend for something mean they said, your strength of forgiveness would go in the "relationships" column. If you stayed focused on your exercise routine, you could add perseverance to

your "physical health" column. Starting to read a funny new book could connect your strengths of curiosity and humor to "leisure."

Step 3: Record any examples of strengths in a few words, like "Good talk with friend" or "Went running." Try to make sure that you focus on your *active contributions* to that area, versus events outside your control. For example, you may have had a work holiday that allowed you to unwind, but your specific choices to read, exercise, and talk to friends during that time became the active ingredients of your self-care. Questions to draw these choices out include, "What did I intentionally bring to this area of my life to feel good?" and "In what ways did I care for myself in this domain?"

If you notice one wellness block is emptier than others, review the profile of personal strengths you've been building and see if you can come up with a way you could apply them to that specific area. Let's say, for example, you feel a dip in work satisfaction and you know that you possess a strength in appreciating beauty and excellence. You might look for an opportunity to compliment someone at work for a job well done.

Try not to feel discouraged if you struggle to find strengths or successes in a certain area. It's quite normal for us to have wellness gaps! We are all works-in-progress. It may help to remember that strengths and successes in one area, say relationships, can fill positivity voids in others, like work or financial well-being. The more you try to build wellness by recognizing strengths in each area, the stronger your spectrum of resilience will become.

Reflection Point

Congratulations! You have reached another summit on your positivity journey. You have taken a big step forward—from catching positive events to exploring your strengths and successes. Think of a way to reward yourself! Fighting the negativity bias and paving a positive path, after all, is not easy. This week's six Core Positivity Practices are:

- Identifying and appreciating your role in creating positive events

- Increasing the duration and intensity of positive feelings around accomplishments

- Seeing difficult life challenges as portals into personal strengths

- Prizing small successes in your daily routines

- Hearing your strengths music in the good things that happen

- Deepening your personal strengths with specific examples

How does this sound? Remember, no one expects you to have mastered all of these new skills by the end of the week. The exercises for this week gave you a lot of choice in designing your own strengths and successes workout:

- Dark Climb, Bright Steps

- Magnifying Your Molehills

- Your Symphony of Strengths

- Child's Mind—The Rock

- Strengths Interviewing

- Successes and Strengths Across Wellness Dimensions

Two other practices I'll emphasize are planning get-togethers with your strengths (looking ahead) and making a weekly list of mountains conquered (looking back). Some daily positivity practice, along with a bit of week-in-review work, can supercharge your workouts.

No matter what you try, the overall goal this week is to appreciate the mountains you climbed and reveal your best possible self. On this leg of the journey, my hope is that you discover many positive qualities that make you feel good about who you are. It can help to remember that you come from tough stuff. There is an excitement too in knowing the strengths you carry with you can lead to new, unexpected heights.

The Full Heart
Cultivating Gratitude

I would maintain that thanks are the highest form of thought, and that gratitude is happiness doubled by wonder.   —Gilbert K. Chesterton

A grateful heart is one filled with an awareness of life's gifts. A story about a demanding music teacher at a prestigious conservatory and a promising student violinist shows the power of getting in touch with those gifts, which may at times be hard to locate.

This violin student showed glimpses of genius, but frequently did not practice, missed lessons, and ignored instruction. The teacher worked hard with the student, spending extra time with him, thinking she could instill greater discipline with her critical style. After a year, however, the student left the conservatory suddenly and without explanation.

Thirty years later, the teacher had retired after developing a serious health condition that left her in pain most days and visually-impaired. Estranged from her family, she often found herself sitting in the dark, alone, with the exception of a young health aide who cared for her. One afternoon, she heard a knock at her front door.

The aide opened the door to find a thin, unkempt man hunched over, gripping a weather-worn violin case. He shook as he mumbled the teacher's name. The teacher recognized the student's voice immediately and invited him in.

He sat down, carefully took out the violin, and began to play, hands shaking. The notes were squeaky, scratchy, and halting. Sometimes he froze for a few seconds in between strokes, staring into space. When he finished, they sat together in a long silence before the teacher finally said, "That was excellent. You obviously have been practicing since I've seen you last."

The student nodded and mumbled, "Yes, yes."

The teacher invited him to come back the next day to play for her again. This became a routine, with the student giving a similar performance each time. Each time the teacher gave him similar praise: "Getting even better. Wonderful. I haven't heard a more pristine version."

After the student left one day, the health aide turned to the teacher and said, "I know you probably don't want to hurt his feelings, but that was terrible. I mean *really* bad." The teacher replied, "You are only hearing the notes. I am hearing the gift."

The next afternoon, when the student arrived for his performance, the teacher was sleeping. After sitting quietly with the aide for a while, the student said, "I know I play badly, but I don't know what I would do without these afternoons. I am wanted somewhere." The aide replied, "You being here is a great gift. Really. I have never seen her so happy. Yesterday she even called the conservatory and asked if any students were looking for lessons. You have restored her interest in life."

Within their exchanged gifts of appreciation, the teacher and student found renewed feelings of hope, acceptance, and vitality. This week's positivity work will help you discover your own gratitude sources and use them to energize your sense of well-being and resilience. Let's begin by exploring where those gifts reside.

Glass Half-Full

The negativity bias, that tendency to focus on what's wrong, can lead to "glass half-empty" syndrome, where we habitually zero in on what we lack. We can easily get consumed by unfulfilled desires, loss, and times we've failed to measure up to others' or our own expectations. This could take the form of dissatisfaction in a relationship, lack of fulfillment at a job, poor physical health, or difficulty setting aside time for yourself. Frustration about our emptiness can give way to strong feelings of sadness and hopelessness.

Entering a state of gratitude has the opposite effect. When we spotlight the gifts of life, even when they are buried among the negatives, we resonate with what we do have and are more likely to feel contentment, joy, and love.

While gifts always surround us, some are easier to spot than others. Gratitude practice will help us bring these gifts into focus, as it promises to increase our well-being, life satisfaction, hopefulness, and the quality of our relationships (Dickens 2017).

Sometimes the gifts we receive are material in nature, like a salary increase at work, a piece of jewelry to commemorate an anniversary, or a gift card for a birthday. Other times they come in the form of words or actions, like a compliment from a friend or a favor from a neighbor. Some gifts we receive seem transcendent, like recovering from a serious illness, the birth of a child, or finding a life partner. Other gifts may not stand out as much to us, like having a place to live and food to eat. One way we can step into the realm of gratitude is to recognize that *all* gifts matter, regardless of their type, size, or visibility.

Good feelings and thoughts come from acknowledging and appreciating any type of gift, whether it comes from nature, other people, life in general, or ourselves. This week, to cultivate gratitude, we will practice zooming in on objects, moments, activities, interactions, and relationships that fulfill us at the deepest levels.

In Awe of the Ordinary

Think of a time you were astounded by something. Maybe it involved glimpsing a full rainbow after a storm, watching a tightrope walker's perilous but graceful journey, or seeing a majestic mountain rising up to the sky. Whatever it was probably felt larger than life. You sensed the mystery of it and stood in its midst with reverence. In that moment, you were filled with awe.

In many ways, cultivating gratitude is the art of inviting awe into your life. It is the simple act of appreciating things—the ability to identify and admire the positive qualities in yourself, in others, and in the world around you. While gratitude often begins with a simple observation, it extends beyond a neutral or factual understanding. You allow yourself to feel a sense of wonder and amazement, to hold the uniqueness or specialness of this object or experience before you.

Imagine holding a diamond in your palm. You turn it over, noticing each brilliant facet, marveling at how this artifact of Earth refracts light into a myriad of colors. You wonder how something so beautiful came into existence, perhaps feeling fortunate that you are able to be in contact with something of such great value. You appreciate your ability to see and feel this precious stone in your hand.

The purpose of this analogy is not to suggest that gratitude is about having access to expensive things, but rather that there are "diamonds" in everything. There are many things in life that we have not studied under the magnifying glass of wonder—with true appreciation for what we're seeing and how unique it is. This is the kind of wonder we often experienced as children, which now can open the door to gratitude.

What is one thing in your life that has filled you with wonder? Perhaps it is something in nature, the birth of a child, watching fireworks—it could be so many things, both ordinary and rare.

EXERCISE: Transforming Ordinary Life

This week's first Core Positivity Practice asks that you search for the gifts within seemingly ordinary parts of life. This approach starts with taking a fresh look at common activities (Part 1) and objects (Part 2). You will also learn how to channel these transformations into a broader feeling of gratitude.

Part 1: Common Activities

In the first part of this exercise, I invite you to consider what you do every day: showering, eating breakfast, traveling somewhere by car or public transportation, calling or texting someone, watching TV, or any other activity. It may feel unremarkable. You might not think twice about these actions; they may pass through the stream of your day unnoticed. You might shrug and think, *So what? Nothing too special about that.*

Go ahead and catch one of these ordinary activities in your net and rate how thankful you feel in general for this activity, on a scale of 1 to 10. It could be any normal part of your routine. Now spotlight it by answering one or more of the following questions:

- What is remarkable about this activity, even if I haven't thought about it that way before?

- In what ways does this activity improve my life or make it easier?

- Is there a sense of mystery to it? If so, what makes it mysterious?

- How could I see this activity in my life as a gift?

- Is this something that would have been possible a hundred years ago? If not, how does that affect how much I appreciate it now?

- What would I miss about this activity if it were not possible?

After you think about or write down answers to these questions, see if your gratitude level rises. Notice too if the kindling effect takes hold, leading to other positive emotions, in addition to gratitude.

When I answered these questions, I chose to focus on email, something many of us take for granted or even feel irritated by. I found myself in awe of the speed with which these messages travel, crossing thousands of miles in a split second. I appreciated how email makes my job as an internship coordinator possible, and the value of that activity to our counseling students. I felt especially thankful for the ability to "pull back" messages after hitting send, which is so helpful for catching mistakes. Not only did my gratitude rating increase by a few points, but it eased the anxiety I normally feel when thinking about a cluttered inbox. It's easier to deal with clutter if you know the thing that feels cluttered is worth it.

If you were in a negative state of mind before this exercise, did your mood change? In what ways did this exercise transform the meaning of your activity?

Part 2: Common Objects

The second part of this exercise asks that you pick a common object in your environment. See if you can place yourself in the presence of that object, holding or touching it if possible, versus just thinking about it. It could be your phone, a kitchen gadget, a tool or personal care item of some sort—really anything. Spotlight this object in the same way you did with the activity, using one or more of the following questions:

- What kind of knowledge did it take to create this object?

- If this object is something in nature, what processes led to its existence?

- What, if anything, is beautiful about this object?

- How does this object make my life easier? What pleasant aspects does it add to my life?

- What good things come from being able to use this object? Personally? Physically? Relationship-wise? Routine-wise?

- If I didn't have access to this object, what would I miss about it?

As before, see if your gratitude level changes when answering these questions. See if you can allow the feeling of thankfulness to expand and linger as long as possible. Leave the object for a while and come back to it. Notice whether it retains some of those new appreciative meanings.

One object that would work well for this exercise would be a vehicle of some kind—a car, truck, or bus. While we usually take this kind of transportation for granted, spotlight questions enable us to marvel at the technology that makes traveling at high rates of speed possible. You might find new appreciation for being able to get places in relatively short amounts of time—and how that makes your job or connecting with others easier, or how it increases your opportunities to go out and do something enjoyable.

Creating More Opportunities for Awe

You can transform as many ordinary activities or objects as you like. As you practice extending deep appreciation to common parts of your life, you will likely notice an improvement in the overall quality of your daily experience. Feelings like joy, contentment, and love should grow stronger, or occur more frequently, as a result of your effort.

You might want to incorporate more of these gratitude touchpoints into each day. The easiest way is to use the activity and object you spotlighted in these past two exercises.

For example, if you spotlighted your phone in part two, every time you pick up your phone, you can invite a sense of awe by thinking, *This lets me easily connect with the people I love* or *I can stay up-to-date with what's happening in the world.* The more touchpoints you create during your week, the more opportunities you'll have to feel grateful.

Don't worry if your feelings of awe and gratitude are not uniformly strong every time you participate in the activity or contact that object. Remember that the positive journey you are on is a cumulative process. Each activity or object, on its own, may not have an enduring or powerful effect, but together they can provide a substantial lift of positivity.

The Open Field of Gratitude

Appreciating the gifts of the present moment doesn't only involve spotlighting common activities and objects. When you stream experience by watching it unfold moment to moment in real time, you open the "field of now" to feelings of gratitude. Your sense of thankfulness can thrive on anything you choose to draw out of that field, anything happening within you or around you, no matter where you are and no matter what point of life you have reached.

To strengthen your capacity for gratitude, you could randomly pause the stream of experience to search for gifts in the open field of the present moment. This exploration takes place through a simplified process of appreciative inquiry, consisting of a single spotlighting question: "As I look around myself or within myself in this moment, what is something I feel thankful for?"

For this open-field practice, you can turn to your immediate senses for direction—what you see, hear, touch, smell, or taste. You might also scan your overall physical or emotional state for a cue, like feeling relaxed, warm, or calm. Watching the stream of your thoughts or identifying something from your surroundings could serve as a useful jumping-off point as well.

Anything is fair game for a gratitude focus in this exercise. You might want to try it in different settings and situations, to discover the easiest way to enter the open field. If you schedule gratitude checkpoints often enough, tuning into your gratitude frequency should begin to feel more natural. You may even find yourself automatically looking around for something to be thankful for. You could also turn it into a game, keeping track of how many open-field gifts you spot in a day and then trying to exceed that number the next day.

Anthony provides a good example of how you can incorporate the open-field practice into your life.

Anthony's Story: Three Gratitude Checkpoints

Anthony is a caring person, an aviation enthusiast who cherishes his wife and family. In his effort to bring gratitude more regularly into his life, he used the open-field exercise three times a week as the world began to face the broader effects of the coronavirus pandemic in 2020.

His first checkpoint took place late on a Sunday afternoon, as he watched a basketball game at home. While feeling relaxed and entertained by the game, he shifted into a deeply appreciative mindset, thinking about how his wife had arrived home safely from a work trip. He felt thankful for her well-being during such a high-risk time.

Two days later, Anthony started his day with thankfulness for waking up without illness. This built a kind of gratitude momentum that led him to another gratitude checkpoint that afternoon: feeling grateful for having a car as he drove home from work. He spotlighted the freedom it gave him, the satisfaction of having paid it off, and the relief from no longer having the pressure of a bus or train schedule.

By paying closer attention to gratitude in these ways, Anthony became more aware of life's brevity and the importance of appreciating as many moments as possible.

Gratitude Through the Senses

When connecting to the present moment, any of the five senses can be useful pathways into gratitude. Sight, smell, touch, taste, and hearing can all increase the immediacy of that feeling of fullness, boosting your receptivity to life's gifts.

Similar to the open-field exercise, you could pause the stream of experience at any point during your day and follow a single prompt for each sense. In this way, your senses can become gratitude portals. If you have any sensory impairments, choose a sense that is available to you.

Seeing: When I look around, what am I seeing right now that I feel thankful for?

Hearing: As I listen, what am I hearing right now that I feel thankful for?

Tasting: As I eat or drink something, what do I appreciate most about it?

Touching: What sensation is a cause for thanks in this moment?

Smelling: What's something I smell right now that is enjoyable or meaningful?

If a particular sense portal does not reveal a source of gratitude, you can move on to another and/or check back at another time. The sensation of breathing can be a sixth portal into gratitude. To open it, close your eyes, breathe in, and ask yourself, "What makes me grateful for this breath that I take into my body?" The answers will likely lead to additional sources and positive feelings, extending the reach of your thankfulness.

For example, when I use my breath as a portal, I often become more appreciative of my family, thinking, *This breath gives my body everything it needs to survive. Because of this breath, I can hug my son and wife, and be there for them.* Noticing how my breathing connects me with nature leads to feelings of peace and transcendence. Then I become grateful for having *those* feelings.

You will likely see this kindling effect at work whenever you step through a gratitude portal. It helps that these portals always travel with you, available for you to step through no matter what's happening in your life. You can even access more than one portal at a time, for a stronger gratitude effect, as Maricela describes here.

Maricela's Story: Portals of Gratitude

Maricela is a training and development assistant working in the human resources field, someone who greatly values being a mom, positivity, and connecting with nature. She combined the portals of sight and sound one morning while working from home.

Maricela first documented the effects of bringing a thankful focus to sight: "Right now I am working from home and am at my desk. I am thankful for my little home office that faces our front window. I like that I get to look outside throughout the day. A neighbor walks by and we wave at each other and I am grateful we have really great neighbors in our subdivision. My son is next to me doing his school work and I am thankful for him and who he is becoming."

For sound, she wrote, "I hear my mom and my niece in the background and I am thankful for each of them. I am thankful that my son and nieces have a very involved grandmother in their lives. My son is listening to music and I am thankful that we share the love of music."

Maricela remarked that sensory gratitude helped her focus on the positives of working from home. She also noticed that opening her senses in this way made the day more pleasurable.

While sensory pathways help us connect with present-moment gratitude, life review is an appreciative process of looking into the past.

EXERCISE: Thankfulness in Looking Back

In a life review, you search for the lighthouse events that have illuminated your path across a larger segment of your life. Powerful sources of gratitude often exist within those events: people you've received help from, life milestones like getting your first job, or falling in love. You can look back at the past few years of your life or reach back as far as childhood.

People often think about life reviews in terms of bringing peace at the end of life, but they can be useful in cultivating gratitude at any age, especially if your current circumstances are stressful or filled with pain. Sometimes the challenges of life demand that we become "gratitude archaeologists." This is especially true if you have encountered major difficulties or traumatic losses along the way, such as losing your home or losing a loved one.

To conduct a life review, you would stream backward across the years and spotlight the biggest gifts that rise into your awareness. These questions can guide your exploration:

- Who has been a gift to you in your life so far?

- What was a wonderful but unexpected surprise in your life?

- Think of an obstacle you overcame. What or who helped you get past it?

- What is one thing you are happy that you learned in life?

- What is one part of your personality that has helped you succeed in some way?

- What is one strength you possess and how has it helped you in life?

- Has anything happened to you that has seemed like a miracle? If so, what was it?

- If you believe in God or a higher power, how has this presence helped you over your lifetime?

The answers to these questions likely reveal the same kind of lighthouse moments you searched for in Week 1.

Another way we can look back for gratitude is to create a list of all the gifts you can remember receiving, as many as you can think of. Include any related to family, friends, pets, accomplishments, school, work, and any other area. Search your life from your earliest memory to the present. Your goal is to create as exhaustive a list as possible.

When you are done, read through the entire list. How does seeing this inventory of gifts affect how you view yourself, the world, or other people? See if you can allow a feeling of full-heartedness to bloom within you. Also notice if reviewing the list increases how hopeful you feel about the future, which can happen when you adopt an abundance mindset.

You might decide to keep this list somewhere where you'll see it often. You could even make a habit of reading it each morning to start your day, and add to it as you think of more examples throughout the week.

Gratitude from the Inside Out

So far, you have created new internal pathways to thankfulness through everyday activities and common objects, through contact with the present moment and your senses, and over the broader landscape of a life history. Like a tree, you have set down strong roots into gratitude's earth, drawing its nutrients through these exercises into your mind, body, and spirit. Well-nourished trees have branches that extend outward, giving the oxygen of their leaves back to the world, sharing their beautiful greenery while offering refuge and shade.

Similarly, you may feel a natural impulse to share appreciation for the gifts you have absorbed with the very people and things that have provided them. Just as the experience of gratitude can reshape your internal life in positive ways, it can have an equally powerful effect when you channel it out into the world.

How about we pause here to take a closer look at that effect? Ready for a brief thought experiment?

- Think of a time you said thank you to someone.

- Why did you thank them? What was their reaction?

- What was it like to send that feeling of gratitude out into the world? How were you affected?

I recently thanked a close friend for inviting me into a writing group he started. It felt good to acknowledge his thoughtfulness, and to share the impact of the invitation, since participating in the group sparked my own creativity. I didn't need him to say anything back. By simply sending gratitude outward, I was honoring his friendship. That felt like enough. Did you discover something similar in your thought experiment?

Most of us display extraordinary effort in many areas of life—as a parent, student, boss, coworker, friend, citizen, caretaker, or in any number of other roles we may take on. If you were to ask people why they work so hard in these roles, few would probably say, "So someone will thank me for it." In other words, we often do what we do for the value of the activity and its meaning, rather than for an acknowledgment of our efforts. Volunteering at a soup kitchen or taking care of an ill family member are good examples of that. This is why some people feel much more comfortable *giving* thanks than *receiving* it.

In other situations, it can feel incredibly affirming when someone expresses sincere appreciation for something you did, especially when you don't expect it. For example, cleaning common areas in your home may be something you do routinely, but a quick thank you from someone else who lives there could feel terrific. You could easily feel closer to that person and want to continue being thoughtful in that way. Research supports that the expression of gratitude is indeed tied to stronger relationships (Amaro 2017; Park et al. 2019).

Researchers Jessica Navarro and Jonathan Tudge (2020) have made the point that deeper forms of gratitude expression do not involve a feeling of obligation, like thanking someone just to obey a societal norm, or returning a favor.

Unlike these more superficial forms of gratitude, *connective* gratitude is the appreciation you express for another person's actions, words, or identity because you value the bond you share with them. Thanking a friend for helping you move or a colleague for supporting you during a difficult time falls into that category.

Expressions of connective gratitude evoke closeness, affection, love, generosity, altruism, and empathy. These expressions say, "You are special to me," and "I am glad you are here with me in this moment." The gratitude exercises ahead will focus on strengthening this form of connectivity.

EXERCISE: Child's Mind—Grati-Notes

This week's child's mind exercise offers a fun way to strengthen connective gratitude. To prepare for this exercise, get two packs of brightly colored sticky notes, of two different colors. Give one pack to someone you care about and whose space you share. It could be a coworker, family member, partner, child, or spouse.

Step 1: Both of you will create ten to fifteen gratitude notes—brief expressions of thanks directed toward the positive actions or attributes of the other person. Your notes could also address a positive aspect of your shared environment, or the spirit of partnership between you, such as, "I am grateful that we've worked so well together in organizing our apartment."

Step 2: After you write your notes, keep their content to yourself. Over the next week or two, place a note each day where your Grati-Note partner is likely to find it. Ask them to do the same for you. You will be able to tell the note is meant for you by the color. Common posting spots are bathroom mirrors, desk drawers, windows, TV screens, and doorknobs. Anywhere can work. The more you can make the note a surprise to find, the more fun the activity will be.

Step 3: Once all the notes are found, sit down with your partner and talk about what positive thoughts and feelings this exercise created. See if it brought you closer in some way, and whether it might have a lasting positive effect on your relationship.

Messages of thanks, when shared in this way, tend to spark lots of positivity. I've seen people cherish the notes they receive through this exercise, keeping them in places where they'll see them often, like on their computer monitors and mirrors.

Now let's take a look at some other ways to ignite appreciation.

Small Sparks of Appreciation

We can express gratitude in passing, casually and spontaneously, such as thanking someone for holding a door open or letting us go ahead in line. These small expressions happen every day and we may not think twice about them.

Any effort to improve the experience of another person presents an opportunity for appreciation. Small forms of gratitude, even if brief and scattered randomly throughout our interactions, warm the environment of connection. These "sparks" may not seem like much, but they can leave auras of happiness. They can strengthen our affection for those we know well and inspire kindness toward strangers.

You might choose to communicate thankfulness in action, words, body language, gifts, or some combination of these. Whatever gratitude language you prefer is fine. Remember that even if your gratitude language is material in nature, like giving someone money as a thank you, it still can count as connective gratitude. When you keep its deeper meaning front and center in your mind, you honor the bond this exchange represents.

Pick a day this week and keep track of your gratitude expressions. You can use your positivity catcher to note them as you go, or gather your gracious moments in a single sitting at the end of the day. A deep-dive inquiry could be revealing:

- When you expressed your thanks, which language did you choose?

- If your gratitude expression fell into more than one mode (action, words, things given, etc.), which mode felt the most powerful or like the best fit at the time?

- What impact do you think your sparks of appreciation had on the other person?

As you review your day or week, you may find some missed opportunities for showing gratitude. Try not to criticize yourself for these oversights, as many forces can drain our gratitude reserve, including stress, time pressure, depression, anxiety, or a challenging life event. Being open to your "misses" can help you better recognize those opportunities when they reappear.

In addition to small sparks of appreciation, you might want to share your thankfulness in a more structured way, as in a letter. Let's see how that could look in this next exercise.

EXERCISE: The Hourglass Gratitude Letter

Feel free to download "The Hourglass Gratitude Letter" worksheet from http://www.newharbinger.com/47858.

Expressing thankfulness in a formal letter can carry us from small flickers of gratitude into a place of concentrated thankfulness, igniting a full-fledged fire of appreciation. The act of writing a letter allows us to approach a source of gratitude with care and sustained attention. We are more likely to embrace past and present gifts in a way that helps us see them in greater detail. This extended form of reflection can expand your range of thankfulness, immersing you in positive thoughts and feelings.

You can write your letter to a person, pet, place, object, or higher power. Your letter may speak to someone you don't know well, someone you love but have had significant conflict with, or someone who you feel almost entirely positive about. It can help you maintain connection with a loved one you have lost, reminding you of the meaningful gifts you received from them and extending the warmth of their presence. The letter could even be addressed to yourself.

The most powerful way to write a gratitude letter is to directly address the person or thing that has helped you in some way. Using the word "you" throughout the letter sustains that connectivity, keeping the channel open.

The hourglass technique can guide your exploration as you write the letter. Following the shape of an hourglass, you begin with an all-encompassing look at reasons for feeling thankful. Here you want to gather everything and anything that contributes to your gratefulness for whoever or whatever you are speaking to:

Dear ,

I am grateful to you because...

The middle part of the letter "narrows" by focusing on a single event, moment, interaction, or way of being that had the most profound effect on you. Maybe you received a perfectly timed supportive phone call at a low point in your life, or maybe a teacher devoted extra time to helping you overcome a learning challenge. Here you zero in on the "peak nourishment" received:

The thing that affected me the most was when you...

The last part of the letter widens again to describe the enduring effects of this positive influence on you and your life, particularly in the present. In the above examples, you might consider how that phone call stopped self-destructive choices you were making, which led to your current capacity for love, or how your teacher's devotion resulted in increased confidence, which became critical to your career success. The final prompt is:

Because of you, I am now...

Remember that this hourglass approach is just one way of doing it. You can, of course, write the letter in whatever way you like. What's important is that it captures your voice and feelings.

While it is entirely up to you whether you would like to share your letter with someone, hearing the words you have written out loud or letting someone read them can create a positive "echo effect." It turns up the volume on the thoughts and feelings you expressed, making them even more impactful, both for you and the listener.

If possible, share the letter with the person you addressed, either reading it to them or allowing them to read it silently. If you wrote the letter to someone no longer living, you might want to read it aloud or share it with someone else so they can witness those powerful thoughts and feelings. You could also share it with a group you are already a part of, or organize a gratitude letter night where others can participate.

You might choose, on the other hand, to keep your letter private, which is fine too. If you do want to keep it to yourself, you can still observe whether having written the letter changes the quality of your relationship in any way. Do you notice yourself acting or feeling any differently toward that person? Does it affect your mood and thought processes, or help you catch more positivity throughout your day?

You could also use your letter as a gratitude reminder, keeping it somewhere you're likely to see it. You could read it periodically, or add to it over time. Sometimes the letter feels so powerful that even touching it can bring up positive emotions and fill your heart with the gifts it highlights.

Brenda offers a compelling example here of how a gratitude letter can capture the best parts of friendship.

Brenda's Story: Honoring an Important Friendship

Brenda is a down-to-earth twenty-seven-year-old who prizes her friends, family, cats, and nature. She wrote her gratitude letter to her close friend Alley, thinking about how lucky she was to have such a good friend in her life. The process ignited feelings of pride, joy, awe, inspiration, and serenity. She felt love when sharing it with her friend, excited that it made Alley feel happy as she faced a difficult time in her life.

Dear Alley,

I am grateful to you because for years, you have shown me endless kindness and an unconditional love that I only ever associated with family. I have always appreciated your friendship and I don't think I tell you that enough. I appreciate that you always pick up the phone to chat and that you know just what to say when I am down about something. I appreciate how much I can count on you. You have always been my voice of reason and someone whose opinion I value. I am grateful to you because you give the best advice and guidance that I could ask for from a friend. You are consistent and you stay true to yourself—some of my favorite things about you. We are in sync with each other in a way that I think is rare to find in life. My college roommate, my travel buddy, my best friend—I am grateful that you are in my life.

The thing that affected me the most, in a good way, was when you turned to me at Danielle's wedding during her father-daughter dance and you told me, "I am going to make sure you have a wedding like this." In that moment, I was feeling down. The wedding was so beautiful and there was so much of her family there. And while I was beyond happy for our friend, I was sad thinking about the fact that my mom and my dad won't be at my wedding. Just sad for my family in general. Without me saying a word, you leaned over, and you told me that. I wondered how you knew exactly what was going through my head. Maybe you don't remember this now because it was just a moment, but it's something that I won't forget. You are my family, Al.

Because of you, I am now more confident and sure of myself. I believe that you had a major role in who I am today. You motivate me to make my life and myself better. You have helped me in ways that I could never repay you for.

I'm not sure how to end this except to say thank you. Thank you for being you and thank you for being my friend.

Sincerely,

Brenda

Roadblocks to Gratitude

Bringing gratitude into everyday life is not always an easy task. Stress, loss, and responsibilities can all interfere with our connection to a spirit of thankfulness. When you're feeling wronged or hurt by someone, for example, it can be harder to think of times you received kindness. The passing of a loved one can fill your heart with such pain that it crowds out appreciation for other things. Giving so much to others throughout your week—to family, work, and friends—can make it difficult to see what is given to you. Battling chronic pain or another health condition might consume the emotional energy you might have otherwise put toward expressing thanks. Worrying a lot can drain that energy too.

Our thoughts can block gratitude as well. We can make "all-or-nothing" assumptions, which are common with depression, such as *I have nothing at all to feel thankful for.* These negative thoughts can be about ourselves, others, and the future. Examples include *I don't deserve anything good, Most people are unkind,* and *The future looks dark.*

How about we pause here to explore your most likely gratitude roadblocks? This is the first step in being able to navigate around them. Let's also answer a few questions, to begin to look at solutions:

- What stops or limits your gratitude impulse the most? Negative life events? Difficult interactions with others? Ways you think about the things that happen to you?

- What might help you get through your roadblocks? Is there an exercise you've already tried from *A Happier You* that could change how you feel?

- In the past, when you felt grateful, what opened the door to that feeling?

Let's say you've found that conflict with others puts up a lot of gratitude roadblocks. You could develop a plan to improve your relationships that includes more active listening. If thoughts are the main obstacle, you could begin to challenge them by asking, "How do I know that for sure?" You could also meet any of these roadblocks by stepping into the meadow of acceptance. You could say to yourself, *I see this roadblock to gratitude is here. I am not going to push against it. Instead, I will wait patiently for it to pass.*

When you feel ready, you can try to pivot from acceptance toward gratitude. As you recall, in the open field, you are reaching for anything that could be a gift. You could enter that field with a thought like *Even though I am feeling down and stressed, one thing I am thankful for is…*

Alternatively, you could begin with self-compassion: *I am having a hard time right now. I understand that I am in pain and suffering. Is there anything within this very challenging moment that I am glad is here? What's one thing I do have going for me?*

As you explore your roadblocks, you might discover that positive emotions and social fulfillment are good gratitude door–openers. When we feel happy and enjoy who we are with, we often can see the gifts of life more clearly. Other parts of this program, like humor, strengths, and love, can also help open those doors, by generating strong positive feelings. You may want to shift your focus to these areas if you are consistently hitting a wall or not having success with the above roadblock-busters. If you do shift focus, keep a lookout for doors into thankfulness, so you can be ready to step through them.

Before we move forward, I want to stress the importance of having realistic gratitude expectations. Including gratitude in a positivity program does not assume you will or should be in a continuously grateful state. The goal of this week is to increase the frequency with which you make contact with the gifts of life, even just a little bit. One small extra moment of gratitude counts as a success! You may find these moments more easily at times by directing gratitude inward. That's where we are going next.

Self-Appreciation

When life becomes difficult, we are more likely to take our personal strengths, successes, and other positive qualities for granted, or not notice them at all. In the spirit of deepening your self-appreciation, you may want to refer back to some of the strengths and successes you identified in Week 2. You can also look for ways you have been coping well with stress. Asking yourself the following questions could be a good starting point:

- As I struggle with this, what's one action I've taken that I appreciate?

- What is one thing about who I am that I'm thankful for?

- One way of showing myself appreciation in this moment is...

- I am grateful for how I...

- In spite of my difficulty, one aspect of my physical being that I feel thankful for is...

- What is one way I have tried to make others happy, even with my limitations?

- Today I deserve a thank you for...

You can bring grateful thoughts toward yourself at *any* time, not only when encountering roadblocks. Organizing this self-appreciation practice by different categories may help, especially if you are having trouble finding something to feel thankful for in the open field. Our positive social, emotional, spiritual, physical, and creative sides can offer unique contributions to our gratitude sourcing:

Your **social self** includes positive self-initiated actions with others, especially how you contribute to your family, friends, and community.

Your **emotional self** encompasses any positive emotional aspects of your being and where your feelings have served you well.

Your **spiritual self** is your capacity to connect with something greater than yourself and includes your appreciation of beauty.

Your **physical self** captures all the good things about your body, how it sustains you and heals.

Your **creative self** consists of anything special you have created in your life, past or present.

In cycling through these areas, you could use a pattern that resembles a mantra or meditation: "I am grateful for my social self in the following ways…" "I am grateful for my emotional self in the following ways…" and so on. Just seeing the wonderful complexity of who you are can inspire a greater overall feeling of self-appreciation. If you can thank yourself for one thing every day, you are well on your way to making gratitude a habit.

The Gratitude Spot

In addition to turning inward, another good way to make gratitude a daily habit is by finding a physical home for it. That home could be anywhere you find yourself during the course of your day—a room, chair, bed, car, or any number of places. The idea is fairly simple. Any time you go to that location, you will attempt to make contact with thoughts and feelings of thankfulness. At first, it may take some reminders, but if you repeat this practice in that spot often enough, your presence there should begin to automatically evoke a gratitude mindset.

You can turn any location into a gratitude oasis. You also can develop more than one. To pick a spot, first think of your weekday and weekend routines. Do you take a daily walk in the morning or evening? What about regularly traveling from one place to another? Perhaps you have a quiet location in your home where you spend some time each day. You might select a comfortable chair in a favorite room, or your bed. You could look outside your home as well. Christine, a Happier You participant, brought her gratitude practice to a relaxation room at her workplace.

Since you want this to become a routine practice, your spot should be somewhere you can visit often. For example, hiking in a state park twenty miles from where you live may be perfect in some ways for gratitude practice, but you may only be able to get there once a month. You should also feel comfortable closing your eyes in your special place and turning off your phone, so you can remain undisturbed for a little while.

Remember that the duration of your gratitude contact can be brief. Even just a few seconds—a single thought even—can trigger a positive shift in your emotional state.

My spot is a chair at a small table where I sit to put in my contact lenses. This works best for me as a gratitude spot early in the morning, before anyone else is awake. I know I have to be at this spot each day, and in these quiet moments, I direct my gratitude spotlight toward one or more areas of my life.

Here are some additional recommendations for getting the most out of your gratitude spot this week:

Prepare: Note a specific time of day you plan to be there and an approximate length. Decide ahead of time how you will access gratitude, whether through a present-moment technique or some other way. Before you reach your spot, rate how grateful you feel, and your stress level, on a scale of 1 to 10.

Practice: Make an effort to reach that spot at least once each day of the week.

Review: After each visit, reflect on how visiting your gratitude spot affected you. Rate yourself again on the gratitude and stress scales after you complete your visit. Here are some questions that could help you spotlight the effects:

- How did getting into a thankfulness mindset change the tone or feeling of that place?

- Did my gratitude-spot time positively affect my interactions with others? If so, how?

- What were the effects on my emotional well-being? Did I notice any positive changes in my mood? If so, how long did they last?

- If I encountered stressful moments or events during the week, did my gratitude spot visits help me manage them? If so, how?

For Christine, spending time in her gratitude spot at work helped her cope with her chronic illness and became a revitalization point.

Flexibility is key! If one spot isn't working well for you, don't hesitate to try another.

EXERCISE: The Stepladder of Gratitude

As your gratitude practice progresses, you may notice you can more easily open yourself to thankfulness. You might feel comfortable with one approach, like open-field practice, or prefer to hop between a few of them. It is not necessary that you master every exercise presented here. My hope is that you find the right fit for your needs.

The final option on this week's menu is a more advanced gratitude practice, called "The Stepladder of Gratitude." In this exercise, you sequentially move from internal points of appreciation to external ones, widening your gratitude focus as you move up the ladder. To listen to this exercise rather than reading it, you can download the recording at http://www.newharbinger.com/47858.

Rung 1: Breath

For a moment, tune into your breath. See if you can feel thankful for your body's ability to breathe, and for what each breath gives you.

Rung 2: Basic Needs

As best you can, take a moment to connect with gratitude around a basic need of yours that has been met. This could be related to housing, clothes, food and water, a source of income, or the air you breathe.

Rung 3: An Action I Took

Now think of a positive action you've taken recently that you are glad you took. See if you can experience thankfulness for the wisdom and effort in you that led to that action, as well as its beneficial effects.

Rung 4: Someone in My Life

Bring to mind someone who you care about and who cares about you. Connect for a moment, in any way you'd like, with gratitude for their presence and what they have brought to your life.

Rung 5: Something That's Happened in My Life

As you look into the past, see if you can bring into focus something that happened that you feel grateful for.

Rung 6: Something in the Broader World or in Society

Letting your field of attention expand, connect with someone or something in your broader world that gives you a reason to be grateful. It could be your work or family, or could extend as far as your community and country.

Once you get to the top of the stepladder, observe your thoughts, feelings, and physical state. You might want to write about some of the effects. What positive emotion signposts can you identify? Was one rung more difficult than the others? If so, how might you improve your contact on that one?

At first, you may want to ascend the ladder slowly, as you learn what each rung asks for, spending longer on more challenging rungs. Over time, you could try climbing at greater speeds, lingering on each rung for only a few seconds or so. Later in your practice, you can try to internally "accumulate" a momentum of thankfulness, collecting the positive feelings of each rung as you move toward the top.

At the top, you can embrace thankfulness as a whole, across the entire landscape of your life and world. Holding each rung's "notes" together in your mind at the top may require some effort, but the more notes you have there, the stronger the chord of gratitude will sound.

Strengthening Wellness Through Gratitude

One of this week's main themes has been the link between cultivating gratitude, connecting with others, and continuing to feel good during tough times. In short, gratitude is an essential part of our ability to manage difficult situations and maintain our wellness footing.

After Hurricane Katrina, police officers in New Orleans faced incredibly stressful conditions. Nearly one-third of these officers later reported symptoms of depression (Bernard et al. 2006). Erin McCanlies and colleagues (2018) studied how gratitude and social support affected their depression levels. They found that the officers who felt more grateful in life had higher levels of social support, less depression, and higher life satisfaction.

How exactly might gratitude help us bounce back? It is likely that gratitude practice will open our hearts to others in ways that make it easier to develop caring bonds. Our hearts are full in those thankful moments, so there is less of a tendency to focus on flaws and deficits—in both ourselves and those around us. This can also protect us from the effects of stressful life events.

Gratitude expression, social support, and feeling good are interconnected. Each strengthens the other. Together, they can make you feel more confident that you can weather the storms of life.

We can also use gratitude practice to fill the seven wellness reservoirs we explored in Weeks 1 and 2: relationships, physical health, leisure, knowledge/creativity, work, finances, and spirituality. Directing thankfulness toward each area can contribute to an overall feeling of life satisfaction, which in turn makes it easier to endure the tough times.

So what would this look like? In many ways, this practice follows the format of the Stepladder exercise, in which we used questions to bring gratitude forward in a sequential way. Here, you are bringing it forward in one wellness area after the other. You could think on the prompt "Something I am thankful for in _____ is..." You would fill in the blank with each wellness category, in any order you choose. How about giving that a try now?

If you find yourself coming up empty in one of the areas, feel free to skip it and focus your question on the others. The emptier categories may show up as a guide. Perhaps, after a recent job loss, you can't think of something in this area to appreciate. Mentioning it to a friend or loved one, they might point out how you now have an opportunity to pick a new career direction, if you so choose. In this way, cultivating gratitude can be a shared experience. Sometimes we need a fresh perspective to help our flowers bloom.

On a final note, let's step out, once more, into the open field. Is there something you are feeling thankful for after reading this chapter?

Perhaps it's the effort you've shown in your commitment to personal growth, the fact you have taken another *Happier You* step along your path of positive living. Your effort radiates outward, lifting all of us in immeasurable ways as it spreads out into the world. And that's something we all can feel grateful for!

Reflection Point

This week you have spent your energy and attention on bringing forward the gifts in life, bolstering your appreciative skillset. Take a moment to admire how far you've come! This week's six Core Positivity Practices are:

- Seeing gifts in the ordinary parts of life

- Tuning into the fullness of present-moment experience

- Looking back for gratitude

- Building connective gratitude

- Appreciating yourself

- Integrating gratitude into your daily routine

Gratitude practice does not have to be complicated or take up a lot of time. Even a small increase in the number of appreciative checkpoints throughout your week can make a big difference in how you feel. Here are the six exercises you have to choose from as you build gratitude into your days:

- Transforming Ordinary Life

- Thankfulness in Looking Back

- Child's Mind—Grati-Notes

- The Hourglass Gratitude Letter

- The Gratitude Spot

- The Stepladder of Gratitude

Other practices you may want to integrate into your week are stepping out into the open field, appreciating yourself more fully, and finding gratitude through the senses. You can use these as drop-in practices, cultivating thankfulness briefly and informally by asking yourself questions like, "What am I thankful for right now?" "What sense can I channel appreciation through?" and "What's one thing I did for myself today?" You can also invite feelings of fullness into a different wellness area each day.

There are so many possible combinations of practice, but they all direct you toward one goal: beginning and ending each day with a heart filled with good things about you and your life.

The Lightness of Being
Finding Laughter and Playfulness

Let laughter and a sense of humor bloom where you are planted and watch the joy you bring to yourself and others.   —Terry Paulson

In ancient Greece, philosophers like Aristotle and Thomas Aquinas saw how humor and playfulness rejuvenate us. To them, laughter and play gave the soul some much-needed rest. It was a way of hitting the reset button.

Have you ever noticed that for yourself? Have you ever felt released from the weight of the world by laughing with a friend or watching a funny movie?

If you have, you wouldn't be alone. Not a lot has changed about the importance of lightheartedness in two thousand years. In fact, with the heavy stresses of our lives, we now need this lighter side more than ever.

Many of us wish we could spend more time on that side of life. With our lives jammed with back-to-back meetings, family responsibilities, and problems to be solved, it's hard *not* to be serious. This is why A *Happier You* has a whole week devoted to removing those weights. We will soon begin to look for the airy spaces hiding inside this intense drama of life.

Thankfully, we came into the world with an instinct to laugh and play. According to one study, two-year-olds laugh, on average, eighteen times an hour, which could add up to over two hundred laughs a day (Nwokha et al. 1994). There is no doubt children see the world with newness and delight. The fields in which they play feel timeless. There, they are unbothered by the difficulties of the past or worries about the future. We can learn a lot from this point of view.

That is why our work this week will focus on stepping back into that place, asking our inner child to come out and play. As Terry Paulson points out, there is great joy here, waiting for you to discover it.

Feel like going there now? If so, let's begin by drawing lightness out from wherever it may be hiding.

Bringing Lightness Forward

Think about a time you laughed so hard you couldn't catch your breath. Maybe you were playing a silly game with someone, or you were unexpectedly caught in a ridiculous situation. Bring it back as vividly as possible by streaming it. Who was with you and what was around you? When you were in that place, how much were you concerned about the past or future?

As you stream this moment, you are bringing the lightness of being into the present. You may even feel like you want to laugh right now. In all likelihood, you weren't worrying much in the moment you've chosen to stream. But what did you notice by going back there? What thoughts or feelings came up?

It's important to honor *any* kind of reaction. Perhaps you learned that letting go through humor and playfulness was a wonderful release. Or maybe you held back in some way. You could have grown up in a serious home, where the lighter side of life was discouraged. Or you could have suffered a traumatic event at some point, which might have diminished your contact with it. Maybe you realized that you don't step into those light spaces often enough, but would like to.

To continue your exploration, take a moment to complete this thought:

Some things I believe now about laughter and playfulness are…

Some responses might be: "It's good for me," "I feel guilty when I have a good time," "They are very far away," and "I laugh a lot, but I could be more playful."

Whatever your attitudes about lightness are, I'm just happy that you are willing to take a look at them—it's a good first step as we begin this part of our journey. You can also, if it's helpful, download the "Bringing Lightness into the Present" worksheet from http://www.newharbinger .com/47858.

I do hope you might consider some of the advantages of welcoming in lightness as we move ahead, but I also recognize the importance of being sensitive to your unique needs and personal history around this topic.

So, I won't ask you to change your beliefs if you have some hesitation, or ask you to dive into lightness if you aren't ready. One of the most important things to me is that you accept yourself *as you are*. Don't pressure yourself to feel something that just isn't coming to you, and don't feel bad about what you do or don't feel.

That being said, you might be surprised by what you do feel if you begin to step more consistently into lighter realms. So, where can we find life's lighter side? Here are some possible places:

- **Surprises:** unexpected events that delight you, such as a surprise party, a funny picture you rediscovered, or the funny comment of a friend during a serious situation

- **Absurdities:** things that don't really make sense but that strike you as funny, such as nonsense words or strange things, like a dog wearing a tutu or a robot whose only purpose is to deliver toilet paper (believe it or not, there was such an invention, called the Charmin RollBot!)

- **Silliness and Play:** anything that is playful and childlike, such as making weird sounds, playing hide-and-go-seek, building forts out of pillows and blankets, or dancing to the soundtrack of a commercial

- **Conversations with Others:** talking to others about everyday things often leads to laughter and lightness, especially if that intention is present

We may find these sources at home, work, and school. We may stumble upon them when least expected, even during deeply serious times. We can watch for them, spotlight them, and even make them a planned destination.

Before we head there, though, I need to stress that any use of humor and play should be kind, loving, and respectful. It should never come at someone else's expense. What *we* see as funny and light, others may not. So if you have any doubt whether something will be well received, whether it is a thought, picture, joke, or something else, I suggest that you pause and think carefully before sharing it. You might also want to ask the person you intend to share it with what their reaction might be.

But in the end, as long as you move into lightness with a good heart and reflective mind, it should lead you and others into positive places.

Stepping into the Light

As a child, I was very serious and sensitive. In middle school, I remember being worried about poor grades more than I remember having fun. Lightness seemed like something other kids had a much better handle on.

This didn't mean that I had no capacity for humor or playfulness, though. Quite the opposite was true. I loved funny movies, comedians like Steve Martin, and the dry British humor of Monty Python. I laughed, often to the point of tears, with my father while watching those movies or listening to him tell funny stories. We had a great appreciation for the absurd.

What was the lesson in this? When it comes to a sense of humor, appearances can be deceiving. While others saw me as a serious kid, it is what I knew *about myself* that mattered most—namely that I valued lightness a lot. I simply preferred to access that side of myself when alone or with family.

I do think that everyone has a lighter side. There are merely differences in how we come into contact with it and how we choose to express it. For example, you may not like to joke around with others, but you may laugh plenty when reading a funny book. You might like to laugh with one family member, but not another. You may use humor and playfulness as a way of coping with mental health challenges like anxiety or depression. The level of humor and playfulness in our lives can vary widely depending on who we are with, where we are, and what we are facing.

How do you prefer to demonstrate humor and playfulness? See if asking yourself these questions can help:

- Where and when do I feel most comfortable connecting to my lighter side? Where am I least comfortable?

- Is there someone I often laugh with?

- Is there a time and place I tend to feel the most playful?

- On a scale of 1 to 10, with 1 being the lowest volume and 10 being the highest, what volume are humor and playfulness at in my life right now? Do humor and playfulness have different volumes, for me, at this moment?

- How ready am I to *turn up* that volume? What would be some of the benefits?

Perhaps you already see that accessing your lighter side more often could brighten days usually burdened by work and family stress. Or maybe you want an opportunity to let your serious side rest. You might view this week as a chance to more fully develop the lighter side of your personality, or to connect with others through humor.

Before we try the first exercise, let's briefly review some of the research behind the benefits of laughter. You might find that your readiness to enter lighter realms increases as you read.

The Benefits of Lightness

If you can call to mind the last time you laughed, it's likely you'll remember that you felt good while you did. You probably weren't as focused on any body aches or ailments you might have been feeling. Your mood may have shifted from anxiety to contentment. If you thought that laughter was the best medicine, the science would support you.

One study found that people who reported laughing at least once a week had a lower death rate than those who laughed less than once a month (Sakurada et al. 2019). Those who laughed more had a lower risk of cardiovascular disease as well. Laughter also strengthens our immune system and reduces stress levels (Bennett and Lengacher 2009).

Norman Cousins (1979), a famous author and world peace advocate, described using laughter to help manage the painful condition of ankylosing spondylitis. He noticed that he had less pain and could sleep better after watching *Candid Camera* and Marx Brothers films. In his book *Anatomy of an Illness*, he wrote, "Hearty laughter is a good way to jog internally without having to go outdoors."

In addition to boosting physical well-being, laughter improves our social health. Laughing with another person leads to positive feelings, enjoyment, and a greater sense of intimacy (Kashdan et al. 2014). The more couples laugh together, the more positively they view their relationship (Kurtz and Algoe 2015).

You can see how lightness in life keeps us healthy in social, physical, and emotional ways. Why does it have such positive effects?

One possibility is that engaging our lighter side distracts us from negative events, increasing the likelihood of feeling good. It may also increase our acceptance of difficult situations. For example, if you find some humor in getting a flat tire (assuming it hasn't put you in a dangerous situation), you could in a sense "float above" that stress, versus feeling stuck in it. Being silly with your grandchildren may help you forget about severe arthritic pain. You might still have the pain, but you aren't focusing on it as much.

Let's return now to a time you had a good laugh and see how it affected your sense of well-being. To do that, I invite you to make a list of all the ways you felt good in that moment: physically, socially, emotionally, and spiritually. You could then rate the strength of how good you felt in each of those areas, on a scale of 1 to 10. If one of those categories doesn't fit, just skip it and focus on the areas in which you were most affected.

This should give you a better idea of the impact humor and playfulness have on you personally. If your ratings are low, try not to worry! We will work on increasing them through spotlighting.

Now it is time to learn more about what brings lightness into your life.

EXERCISE: Sources of Laughter and Playfulness

A first step toward enjoying more laughter, mirth, and playfulness in life is getting a clearer picture of the fountains from which they flow. We will focus first on humor and what makes you laugh. You will need a sheet of paper and about ten to fifteen minutes of time to yourself.

Your humor fountains can include stand-up comedians, lighthearted movies, board games, and fun activities, among other things. Laughter can pour forth from the silly things your pet does, your own observations about the world, funny people you know, and family members who share your sense of humor. Anything can be a fountain, depending on your sense of humor.

This exercise will ask you to brainstorm as many laughter sources as possible, organized by fountain category. When you are ready, begin by following these four steps:

Step 1: On a sheet of paper, create a column for each fountain, naming it at the top. You could use the following category list:

people in your life, comedians, movies or TV shows, activities, and thoughts or observations. Feel free though to change the actual titles, not include some, and add others. You might want to add, for example, a sixth category for pets or work.

Step 2: As you consider each source, list as many past or present examples as you can. Any time someone or something funny crosses your mind that fits one of your categories, count it! The goal is to make your columns as full as possible, regardless of how much humor each particular source contains. It is perfectly fine too if you want to come back to your list another day to give yourself more time. If you're having trouble coming up with examples, you can also ask someone who knows you well to remind you of things that make you laugh.

Step 3: Once your column lists are complete, draw a line connecting any examples that have something in common. The line can cut across categories. For example, my father is somebody who I laughed a lot with, a comedian we enjoyed together was Robin Williams, and one activity we shared was watching movies he starred in. This step helps illustrate the interconnectivity between the people, things, and situations that bring humor into your life. The more connections you discover, the deeper that source will feel.

Step 4: Select an example from your list to stream. Allow any positive feelings from the sixteen signposts to fill you, as well as any thoughts or related memories that make you smile.

Step 5: Now look at your lists as a single collection. Allow your eyes to scan *all* the items you've identified in *all* of the categories. Does the number of examples you were able to think of surprise you in any way? When you see these items together, what do you make of your capacity for lightness?

As you probably guessed, the goal of this exercise is to make you more aware of how many sources of laughter you can enjoy. Knowing *what* they are and *how* they are connected will allow you to draw from them more intentionally and frequently. I also encourage you to welcome thoughts like, *When I see these lists, I know there are many fountains of laughter available to me.*

If one of your fountains flows less strongly than others, see if you can look at this particular source as an opportunity for humor growth, rather than a permanent deficit. In Week 5's work with enjoyable and meaningful activities, you might plan to try some new activities you think could lead to laughter.

Before we leave this exercise, let's spend a little more time focusing on the fountains of playfulness. Similar to humor, playfulness is about temporarily letting go of the heavy elements of life. You can be playful and not laugh very much, but still feel extremely light.

When you look at children, you can see that opportunities for playfulness abound. They can become our teachers as we follow them into their imaginations through Lego-building, dressing up, or playing tag.

Over the next few days, take note of any desire to be playful, no matter how faint, or any thoughts you have about playfulness. You could use one or more of these gentle prompts:

- When did I feel most carefree today?

- When will there be an opportunity this week to play?

- Who values playing in my life? Will I see them soon?

- How do I feel when I'm playing?

- If I were a child right now, what would I be doing?

The answers that come to mind, such as game nights, coloring, puzzles, playing an instrument, or video-chatting with nieces or nephews, may turn into powerful sources. They may even find their way onto your laughter fountains list.

Throughout this exercise, you are giving yourself permission to step into child's mind. You are telling yourself it's okay to put down the heaviness of adult responsibilities, and that this is not only acceptable, but a necessary "rest" that allows you to accomplish those adult tasks more effectively. If you ran into any difficulties, it could help to see the list you started as a living document, adding new items as they occur to you.

I hope your observer self can stick around too, because now we're going to focus on catching and spotlighting moments of lightness.

Catching Moments of Lightness

Now that you know where your lighter moments like to hang out, it's a good time to use your net to catch them in the stream of life. This is the same streaming and spotlighting practice from Week 1. You'll bring those moments close to you, allowing them to expand more fully into your awareness. That way they can create those delightful positive ripple effects.

These lighter moments can really stand out, especially if we are laughing with others. According to the research, many parts of our brain kick into action at once when we laugh socially (Wildgruber et al. 2013). Our brains also release natural endorphins (Manninen et al. 2017), which are pleasure chemicals that can help us remember what happened more easily (Phale and Korgaonkar 2008).

This is all good news for our lightness-catching work. Laughter isn't required either. In our search, we can include lighter moments that bring us mild amusement, like reading a cartoon or hearing a pun.

Have something in your net right now? Something from the past day or two? If so, press pause on your stream and ask yourself one or more of these spotlight questions:

- What made that funny or amusing?

- How much did the funny or playful moment lift me? And in what ways?

- How far did the effects extend? Into relationships or other situations?

- In what ways did I contribute to creating this moment?

- Which of the sixteen signposts came along with it? What other positive feelings got sparked?

As with your other streaming practices, you can choose to scan a single day or an entire week. You could even stream the present, watching for lightness minute by minute. You might keep your net out as you move forward, ready to hit the pause button once you come upon something funny or playful. The width of the net you cast is up to you. Remember that the more times you cast your net, the more likely you'll find something in it! The very act of searching for lightness can also heighten its importance, as it did for Maya.

Maya's Story: Connecting Through Funny Moments

When Maya practiced catching lightness over the course of a week, the importance of sharing humor with others became clear. The first moment that stood out was a phone call from her mother, a nurse manager at a hospital. Her mother told her that when a patient's COVID-19 test result came back negative, everyone started dancing. Some staff who didn't even know what was going on started dancing too.

"I thought it was hilarious," Maya wrote. "It filled me with joy."

Her other netted moments included watching a video of a tortoise beating a rabbit in a race, which she shared with her friends. She let another friend know about a Netflix comedy. Her friend ended up watching the entire season that day. Maya also laughed at a meme someone had posted on social media.

Maya noticed through all these streams that she had the ability to find funny moments in small things. She also recognized a deep appreciation for how "lightness catching" brought her closer to others in enduring ways. Catching and sharing those moments helped her friends experience feelings of gratitude and enjoyment, mirroring her own feelings. She wrote, "One thing I learned is how contagious positivity can be."

Sometimes streaming a small, funny moment produces a tiny ripple on the positive emotion pond. As Maya's story shows, streaming a series of funny moments, on the other hand, can turn that ripple into a wave. This is the concept of "stacking," gathering light moments together and reliving them in rapid succession.

Humor Stacking

When Maya stacked the funny moments she streamed from her week, she was not only filled with joy, but also reported being able to let go of her stressful thoughts. What's more, replaying these peak positive moments in a single, continuous stream became a kind of fuel for focused action. She found she was able to complete her school assignments with more confidence and less anxiety. Her drive to tackle challenges increased as well, as she noticed being able to complete more tasks on her agenda.

You might try applying this stacking method to your own stream of funny or playful moments and see what the effects are. To do this, it's helpful to keep a record of the moments you find in your net as you encounter them. The positivity catcher notebook is a great place to do that, and you likely only need short descriptions of each moment.

I would recommend keeping your net out for at least four or five days, so you can accumulate a number of moments. After you replay the entire collection, consider the following questions:

- What intensity of lightness do you notice on a scale of 1 to 10?

- How does it affect the quality of your day or energy level?

- Are any other positive emotion signposts activated, like love or gratitude?

If you're having some challenges catching lighter moments or finding enough to stack, this next exercise will show you how you can transform everyday activities into events that bring you amusement or laughter.

EXERCISE: Finding Humor (And Hope) in Everyday Activities

Sources of lightness are all around you, but they may hide in seemingly routine activities, such as brushing your teeth, sweeping the floor, driving, and putting laundry away. In one study, some residents of an assisted living facility said that many everyday situations made them laugh (Westburg 2003). These residents also happened to be the most hopeful.

Why might this be the case? When we find something amusing in things that feel boring or ordinary, like daily tasks around the house, it shows us that we can transform uneventful parts of life into something enjoyable or fun. Suddenly, everything we do on a daily basis is fair game for a lightness makeover.

This exercise will give you some practice with these makeovers. It takes about ten to fifteen minutes to complete and asks that you use your positivity catcher notebook. Ready to try?

Step 1: Make a list of three to five situations you find yourself in every day. Use your morning, afternoon, and evening routines as a guide. They can include getting ready for the day, making a meal, driving somewhere, sending email, talking to a friend, or anything else.

Step 2: For each situation, ask yourself, "What is something amusing or unusual about that?" or "Has that situation ever brought a smile to my face?" For example, when sending a text, you might recognize that your autocorrect inserted the wrong word, which led to it saying something very odd. In doing laundry, you might think about how your cat ended up stealing an article of your clothing.

Step 3: See if you can write down any humorous thoughts or observations that apply to these situations. Imagine if you had those funny thoughts *when* the situation was occurring. Would they have brought a smile to your face?

Step 4: The next time you engage in one of the activities you listed, see if you can find something amusing or funny about it.

Not every ordinary routine or activity will lend itself to something funny. If you run into one that doesn't lighten you in the way you hoped, go ahead and move on to something else. And if you successfully transform some activities, see if that made you feel more hopeful about things being enjoyable or going well.

Now that you've tried this exercise, let's pause for a moment and consider where we are on our lightness journey. Our work so far has mostly centered around the present moment or recent past. You may realize that the amount of light cast by ordinary life may not be very bright, or maybe there's not much to feel light about right now. Is that true for you?

If so, sometimes we need to reach further back into the past to discover sources of playfulness and laughter. Next, we will keep our finger on the rewind button a bit longer to find those deep reservoirs.

Light from the Past

During stressful times, when looking for lightness, it can be helpful to extend your stream to encompass years, as opposed to simply days or weeks. When you open your field of view broadly like this, you are more likely to find those humor lighthouses.

Maybe these were moments in which laughter left you breathless or led to a profound sense of closeness with someone you love. Lightness could have come from a wildly fun outing, or as part of a conversation where everyone laughed to the point of tears. These moments could come from early childhood, but because of their intensity you remember them like they happened yesterday.

Once you find a humor lighthouse, see if you can set aside twenty minutes to write about it. Try to capture in great detail the who, what, why, when, and where of the event. The more detail you add, the more you can intensify its positive emotional impact. As best you can, allow yourself to reexperience any of the positive emotions and thoughts you had during that event. You could pause your writing at any point and close your eyes to stream it. When you finish your writing or visualization, see where it leaves you emotionally.

Are you feeling any more encouraged? Or less affected by current stress in your life? Does it awaken a new direction in you, such as wanting to reconnect with that humor source? Kevin found just such a wake-up call in writing about his humor lighthouse.

Kevin's Story: A Mouse in the Night

Kevin is a forty-one-year-old fundraiser who loves traveling, fitness, and being a part of a large family. For his humor lighthouse practice, he chose a bright memory from his childhood thirty years earlier.

Kevin used to take trips to the Pocono Mountains with a friend's family, and on one such trip, his friend's mother woke up everyone in the night with a blood-curdling scream. She had seen a small field mouse and everyone snapped into action, trying to find it. In the pandemonium, Kevin had grabbed a slingshot to protect everyone from this intruder. They were able to get the mouse outside with no harm done and everyone ended up having a good laugh.

When Kevin looked for the positive emotion signposts in this incident, he found joy, enthusiasm, connectedness, and gratitude. He wrote, "As a young child, I was very ill and had to fight for my life. This is the first time I remember fighting for others, even though it was a mouse. I was determined to protect them from it."

This lighthouse practice also made Kevin realize that most of his
funny memories were in the distant past. It inspired him to become
more intentional about searching for lightness every day.

Creating Opportunities to Laugh and Play

Another way you can invite more laughter and play into your life is by
planning time during the week to *intentionally* open those doors. Just as
you scheduled "get-togethers" with your strengths in Week 2, you would
look for opportunities to activate your sources of lightness. Your lists of
sources and activity transformations from earlier can remind you of all
the different avenues open to you. Then, as you plan for the days or weeks
ahead, you can see what places are open for your lighter-side hangouts.

For example, you could start out each morning searching the Internet
for a funny meme or comic. You could plan dinner conversations to
include a question like, "What's one funny thing that happened to you
today?" You might schedule a funny movie night each week, when you
watch a comedy with someone.

If you prefer to focus on the social side of lightness, you might look for
an absurd thing that happened to you and share it with a friend. If you
have young children, grandchildren, or nieces and nephews, you could
schedule a visit and play a fun game with them. To add even more playfulness into your week, you could sprinkle in card games, puzzles, chess,
painting, storytelling, or anything else that awakens the child in you.
How do these ideas sound?

As an added bonus, any time you work on one of this week's exercises, it counts as a planned date with the lighter side. At the end of the
week, you might want to check your "lightness meter," that 1 to 10 scale,
to see where you end up. If it's lower than expected, you can always make
an effort to plan more get-togethers.

This next exercise offers a more hands-on way you can step into the childlike delight of laughter and play. It will put that inspiration into your hands, quite literally.

EXERCISE: Child's Mind—Lighter Than Air

Your practice this week has focused on bringing the carefree joy of childhood into the present moment. This exercise will guide you in finding an object to transport you into that state of mind and help you sustain your connection to it.

Step 1: Find a portable, lightweight object that represents your lighter side. Examples include a feather, sticker, funny photograph, drawing from childhood, joke written on a slip of paper, a game piece from a favorite board game, a balloon that hasn't been inflated, or a small toy. It could represent something you loved as a kid, like a small action figure from a cartoon you always watched. The more it brings you back to that simple, happy time, the better.

Step 2: Every time you make contact with this object, visually or by touch, see if you can think about a playful or laughter-filled memory. You might say to yourself, *Every time I see or feel this object, I give myself permission to go light.* Aim to make contact at least three times a day, if possible.

Instead of carrying the object with you, you might decide to place it near your computer or in a room where you spend a lot of time. Any way you want to use it is great! Another idea is to create a lightness shrine, a larger collection of objects that represents your child's mind. You could use this shrine as you might use a gratitude spot, planning to visit it once a day, welcoming thoughts about playfulness and humor when you're there. This exercise is another example of how you can make humor and playfulness more intentional.

Now let's take one step further, looking at how these important parts of our experience can help us cope and connect with others.

Using Humor to Bond and Cope

The great comedian Robin Williams once said, "Comedy is acting out optimism." He seemed to be saying that whenever you look for the lighter side of life, you are acknowledging that things can get better. This is especially true during difficult times.

Humor helps put conflict in a more balanced perspective, allowing us to move on from it more easily. For example, sometimes we can find something to laugh about after having a fight with a loved one over something relatively minor. After some time has passed after the disagreement, you might say to each other, "I can't believe we got so upset over something so small!"

There are plenty of stressful situations in life that permit you to step onto the lighter side. One day, as I watched helplessly from the window, storm winds knocked down a large section of our thirty-year-old fence. I said to myself, *Huh, would you look at that. There goes the fence.* Something struck me as funny about that overly calm observation. I noticed that reaching for lightness in that moment blocked stressful thoughts about the cost of replacing the fence. It led to the thought *This too shall pass.*

Finding humor in tough situations tells us something very encouraging about ourselves: we have the power to transform problems into something brighter and more manageable. And if that's true, we can likely reach important goals in life more easily.

As you may recall from Week 2, humor is one of the strengths you can rely on to do that. If you don't see it as a strength when it comes to managing stress, that's okay. It's a skill you can work on throughout the week, just as we have for the other positivity areas. How about we start now?

EXERCISE: Putting Stress in Its Place

This exercise will give you practice in meeting stress with lightness and watching what happens as a result. You will want to have your positivity catcher or something else handy to track your thoughts, and allow yourself the same ten- to fifteen-minute window you've used for other exercises. You would follow these three steps:

Step 1: Think of a mild to moderately stressful time in the past. Stream it, so that you have a good grasp of the details.

Step 2: Ask yourself the following questions:

- Can I laugh at myself in some way related to what happened?

- Was there something absurd, ironic, or funny about it?

- How could reaching for lightness have helped me cope, either during or immediately after the event? Or now, if I still feel upset about it?

Step 3: See if you can write down any humorous thoughts that apply to that situation. For example, someone who had a stressful supermarket outing might write, "I must have looked very funny fighting with that shopping cart in the pouring rain!" You will know if your humor strength is showing if you smile when you write down the thought.

Let's see how this could work. Imagine being woken up by a bird that decides to sing loudly at your bedroom window at five a.m., when you're still trying to get some sleep. To counter your irritation with a bit of lightness, you think, *This bird wants to make sure that I don't oversleep. Who needs an alarm clock when you have a bird!* You find that this thought dampens your frustration and helps you get back to sleep, even with the bird singing loudly.

You might want to try these steps with more than one event to see if you get consistent results. Remember that whatever you choose does not have to be laugh-out-loud funny. After Step 3, you can also test the hope-stimulating power of your work by rating how in-control or optimistic you feel on a scale of 1 to 10.

Some of the most stressful events we encounter involve our personal miscues. There are definitely advantages to laughing at ourselves from a coping perspective; however, I recommend supporting yourself with a caring thought afterward.

For example, if you laughed at how much trouble you had putting together a bookcase, you might follow it up with a thought like, *Yes, building things with lots of steps is not one of my strengths. But I am quite skilled in other areas*, or *We all have moments like that*. This last thought is very true. We all mess up at one point or another. But when we can laugh at ourselves in a loving way when it happens, this turns into another strength.

Before we leave this exercise, I have one last small twist for you: a fourth step.

One of the things we know about humor and playfulness is that they help us feel close to others. Robert Provine (2000), a researcher who spent most of his career studying laughter, found that we are thirty times more likely to laugh in the presence of other people than by ourselves. This finding shows that we use humor and playfulness for connection. It creates a kind of social warmth.

So this fourth step is about bringing out these bonding possibilities. The idea is to share your stressful moment *plus* your humorous thoughts about it with someone. See if they laugh with you. As Provine discovered in his research, laughter is truly contagious, so don't be surprised if sharing it leaves you both in stitches.

Alyson, a graduate student, gives us a great example of how you can laugh at yourself while deepening connections with someone in the process: "For some reason, I tend to eat for sustenance, and not as much for taste or presentation. I also can't bear to throw food away unless it's truly gone bad. Because of this, my partner jokingly refers to me as 'Private,' as in army private, when he sees me eating crumbs, days-old leftovers, something cold out of the refrigerator that is meant to be served hot, or anything else he considers to be inedible. I'm not ashamed of this at all, so I join in with him and laugh about it."

In this example, not taking herself so seriously is one way Alyson increases enjoyment and adds resilience into her relationship.

Lightness in the Fields of Wellness

As you become more skilled in finding the lighter side of life, you may want to practice filtering lightness through each of the seven areas of wellness we have talked about: relationships, physical health, leisure, knowledge/creativity, work, finances, and spirituality. If you are encountering stress in one or more areas, you can ask yourself a question similar to the one in Step 2 of the previous exercise: "Is there a chance to see these difficulties through a lighter lens?" or "How might I bring more playfulness into this domain of my life?"

For example, if work is a point of stress, you might stream your job activities for examples of lightness. You might identify great opportunities to use playfulness or humor to bond with coworkers or your supervisor. (As a reminder, though, make sure that your attempts at lightness won't be interpreted as offensive.) Or if health is a trouble spot for you, you might follow the path of Norman Cousins (1979) and schedule at least fifteen minutes of watching funny shows when you're not feeling well.

If you like, take some time now to ask yourself which self-care area is most in need of some lightness. Then you could use any one of the exercises we have explored so far, while focusing in on this area.

Reflection Point

This week's practices of finding humor and playfulness join a growing self-care tool kit that includes spotlighting positive events, building awareness of strengths and successes, and cultivating gratitude. As you try out these new skills, you are better equipping yourself to access positive thoughts, feelings, and actions. The more you practice, the more you will naturally lean toward the good in life.

As far as your lightness journey, you deserve a lot of credit! It is not always easy to go from heavy to light, and then to bring others into that equation. But because of your courage and commitment, the transformative power of humor and playfulness is now in your hands. The Core Positivity Practices you are working on this week include:

- Revealing your sources of lightness

- Streaming and spotlighting funny or playful moments

- Creating more opportunities to laugh and be playful

- Lowering stress with humor

This week's exercises should show you how the lightness of being "keeps us larger than what we do, and greater than what can happen to us," as it was described by L. W. Kline (1907) in the *American Journal of Psychology* over a hundred years ago. Here is a summary of what's on the week's exercise menu:

- Sources of Laughter and Playfulness

- Finding Humor (and Hope) in Everyday Activities

- Child's Mind—Lighter Than Air

- Putting Stress in Its Place

In addition to these exercises, it might help to incorporate ten to fifteen minutes each day of streaming and spotlighting work, to expand the lighter moments you discover. You may also want to schedule activities with others, to create light moments. Along with streaming, you could practice humor-stacking. Keep in mind too how your wellness areas are benefiting from any and all of this effort.

Here's one final uplifting note. In getting to this point, you may have discovered one of the secrets to *A Happier You*: much of happiness truly does float above you, but you can always make yourself light enough to reach it.

The Engine
Fueling Life with Enjoyable and Meaningful Activities

Happiness is an activity. —Aristotle

In 1953, a thirteen-year-old found a job parking cars in the Italian city of Lucca. When he stepped into one of those cars for the first time and turned it on, he wasn't quite prepared for what happened next. The feel of the steering wheel in his hands and the engine rumbling to life electrified him with excitement.

At the time, his family lived in a refugee camp and their home was a single room shared by other families. One can only imagine the possibilities of speed, freedom, and purpose he felt when that car's engine came alive. This thirteen-year-old was none other than Mario Andretti, who went on to become one of the most celebrated race car drivers in the world. He devoted his life, quite literally, to staying in motion.

This week of *A Happier You* is all about harnessing the same energy that Andretti discovered in Lucca—the positive sparks in what we do every day. Don't worry, you won't need to drive a race car to capture that fire. You can find it in what you already do. Our work together will concentrate on bringing out the positivity within those actions, as well as finding new gears and additional fuels for feeling good.

Happiness and Meaning Through What We Do

Activities and feeling good often go together. Have you noticed, for example, that when you are doing something you enjoy, your overall sense of happiness increases? This connection may seem obvious, but it shows that we usually find happiness when we are active in some way. It comes *through* what we do.

Victor Frankl, a concentration camp survivor, was very much aware of this fact. In his famous 1962 book *Man's Search for Meaning*, he described how meaning in life emerges from the actions we choose. Those actions can include conversations with others, work-related tasks, exercise or sports, and hobbies. They can also be wholly contained within ourselves, like thinking and daydreaming.

Life itself is a set of continuous motions. Each movement is a possible storehouse of good thoughts and feelings. Some activity happens on its own, like our breathing and the beating of our hearts. We can decide when to start and stop other forms of activity, like jogging. Finding control, enjoyment, and meaning in what we do are important ingredients of well-being. Some activities even lead to an optimal state called "flow" where you are "in the zone," totally immersed in the activity (Csikszentmihalyi 2008). As we progress through the week, you will learn how to gain easier access to all of these wonderful effects of being in motion.

How will we accomplish that? We'll look at ways to build enjoyment and meaning into less-desirable tasks like organizing a closet or paying bills. We will also consider new activities that might fuel your body and mind. We'll be spending some time too exploring the connection between your values, goals, and daily activities. This work has the potential to strengthen your sense of purpose and clarify your direction in life. I will invite you to answer big questions like, "Where do I want be five years from now?" I think you might agree that we all could use a well-functioning GPS device in the car of life—our values and goals can guide our daily decisions in this way.

Before we step into that car, how about we check the status of your activity "engine"? Ask yourself the following questions, based on how you are feeling right now. See if you can get a 1 to 10 meter reading on each, with 1 being the lowest level and 10 being the highest.

- What's my current energy level like?

- How much do enjoyable activities fill my days and weeks? How about meaningful activities?

- How much activity balance do I have across areas of my life (work/school, family, social, recreational)? Am I "running on empty" in any of them?

- How much do I want to add new activities into my weekly routine?

- How satisfied am I with the direction of my life? Do I need a course correction?

If your meter readings reflect a relatively low level on any of these questions (5 or lower), it could signal that this week's theme is especially important for you. If you are on the higher end, perhaps you're looking more for a light tune-up than a full engine rebuild.

Before we explore life's activities in greater depth, it might be good to look at some of the roadblocks to activity fulfillment, and talk about how we might get past them.

Finding Pathways to Enjoyment and Meaning

At one point or another, most of us have felt like we've had too few enjoyable or meaningful activities in life. It's normal to hit uneventful periods. For example, becoming an "empty nester" or retiring might leave more space in your days than you would like. And sometimes, the conditions of life just don't leave room for the things we want to do more often.

Sixty-hour work weeks leave little room for hobbies. An unexpected injury can suddenly limit your ability to exercise or play sports.

Depression, anxiety, or grief can also cause these dips. You may have a tendency to withdraw from social and recreational activities after losing a job, while going through a divorce, or when encountering some other major life stressor. Isolating yourself in this way can cut off the positive fuel you might get from being in motion. Low energy and trouble getting started can trigger negative thoughts like *Nothing is enjoyable* and *Why bother trying anything today?* And then thinking this way can leave you feeling even more stuck.

So how can you get out of this cycle, or prevent it from getting worse? How can you respond to a lot of empty space in your days and fight the weight that can keep you from enjoying things?

One way is to step out into the meadow of acceptance, as I've mentioned in previous weeks—to allow these negative feelings and spaces to exist as they are. When we do this, we slow down or even stop our reactions to negative thoughts and feelings that make us feel worse. An accepting mindset makes it more likely that you will take a step toward some positive action as well. It allows negative feelings to pass more quickly, encourages patience, and suggests that you don't need to move any faster than you want.

Another strategy is to look for an ignition switch—something that generates a spark that gets us moving in a more positive direction. This switch can be a very small action, like getting up to take a shower, going for a five-minute walk, or picking up a book and reading at least one page. These small actions may sound easy, but when you have a lot weighing you down, they can feel incredibly challenging.

That's why we need "switch flippers," thoughts that increase the likelihood that we will take that first step. One of my favorites is, *Even though I really don't feel like it, let me try doing this one small thing to see what happens.* Another might be, *If I just start to do something, maybe I can turn around how I feel.*

These thoughts, by themselves, can open a window of hope—even if just a crack. Hope, even in tiny amounts, can then lead to other positive thoughts like *Maybe my day will be better after all.*

What are your "switch flippers"? What thoughts do you typically use to motivate yourself when it feels hard to get going? Take some time now to write down a few or put them in your phone. It's best to keep them somewhere easily accessible, since you never know when you might need them.

If you find you're struggling to come up with ways to flip your ignition switch, you can always turn to Isaac Newton, the famous seventeenth-century physicist. His first law of motion states that a moving object tends to keep moving, and an object at rest tends to stay at rest. The same is true for people.

When you get into a positive action state, you tend to keep going in that direction. As you "get rolling," you also gather other positive actions, thoughts, and feelings that help you continue along your path.

For example, pushing yourself to get out of bed when feeling depressed could lead to spending some time stretching, which may result in eating a healthy breakfast. That breakfast, in turn, could give you more energy and improve your mood. As a result of feeling happier, you might call a friend and make plans for later that day. This positive chain reaction began with the seemingly small decision to get out of bed.

This next exercise will offer some practice in tracing your positive activity chains, while also raising your awareness of the good feelings that go along with them. Ready to begin?

EXERCISE: Your Positive Activity Chains

As you know, some activities move you in more helpful directions than others. In this exercise, we are going to focus only on your positive actions, watching how they lead to other positive actions and feelings. It should take about five minutes and you will need a sheet of paper on which to draw your chain. I suggest starting the exercise in the middle of the day, so you can more easily remember your activities and their effects.

Step 1: You're going to begin your chain from the time you woke up. Ask yourself, "What is the first positive action I remember taking after I woke up?" Jot that down, using about four or five words. Then draw a small arrow pointing down. For example, perhaps you woke up early, which led to a beautiful early-morning walk.

Step 2: Now ask yourself, "What was the *next* positive action that this led to?" or "Because of that, one positive step I took was..." Write down what you noticed in a few words. This is the next link in your positive activity chain. Maybe you found that the early walk led you to have a productive work session.

Step 3: Draw another small arrow down from this level, repeating one of the above questions so that you can create the next link in the chain. Repeat this process until you reach the present moment. In our example, links included being able to take a well-timed break, eating a healthy lunch, spending unpressured time with family because of productivity, and meeting an important work deadline.

Step 4: Review your finished chain and write down one positive feeling connected with each level. You may want to look over the list of sixteen signposts beforehand, to have them fresh in your mind. Finally, ask yourself, "When I see all these connected positive activities and feelings, what can I conclude about myself, the world, or my future?" Your positive activity chain could imply a variety of enduring personal strengths, which could be connected to your future success across many areas of life.

This exercise has hopefully shown you how you can use the power of Newton's first law to boost your activity momentum. The more positive chains you can trace, the more control you should feel over your positive emotion momentum. A good goal would be tracing three chains over the week. You can also try this exercise to combat low moods. If you do, you could build your chain in real time, adding new links as they arise throughout the day.

So far, we have explored how igniting positive activity momentum is helpful when establishing a stronger foundation for feeling good. Now let's spend some time talking about the types of fuel your engine needs to run well.

The Fuel of Enjoyment and Meaning

There are two main types of activity fuel: enjoyment and meaning. Some activities may bring you enjoyment, but not much in the way of deeper meaning. Eating ice cream, playing a board game, riding a roller coaster, and watching a sitcom could fall into that category. Other activities are full of meaning, but seem less pleasurable. These can include helping a friend move, volunteering for a community clean-up, studying for a major exam, or providing assistance to someone in need. Our sense of well-being depends on having both kinds of fuel. You may notice, however, that you have more of one kind in your life right now.

For example, if you devote all your waking hours to helping others in crisis amid harsh conditions, each day may carry great meaning, but not offer much in the way of pleasure or comfort. The opposite could be true if you have an easy summer job at the beach, which allows you to go out with friends every night—a more obvious source of pleasure than meaning.

Of course, pleasure and meaning rest in the eye of the beholder. Someone committed to service may derive great enjoyment from improving the lives of others. Likewise, that summer beach job can hold a tremendous amount of meaning for someone who loves the ocean.

The most enjoyable and meaningful activities in your life can also be the most absorbing. Can you think of a time you felt like you "lost yourself" in something enjoyable? Maybe it was while playing music, competing in a sport, painting, writing, or doing a puzzle. You might consider these your passions. According to Csikszentmihalyi (2008), you know you're getting into this kind of "flow" when you are:

- Challenged at a high level

- Able to concentrate in an intense and focused way

- Not feeling self-conscious

- In control

- So absorbed that time feels like it speeds up or slows down

- Engaging in the activity for its own sake

Of course, the activities that create flow aren't fixed. You can always enhance the flow qualities of what you do. The mindfulness, streaming, and spotlighting practices you are learning could help, since they immerse you in the present moment. Questions like "How can I make this activity more challenging?" and "How can I increase my focus while doing this?" are also great springboards into flow.

Ready for a short activity? This one is designed to help you find your sources of enjoyment, meaning, and flow.

On a sheet of paper, make three columns, one for enjoyable activities, one for meaningful activities, and one for activities that are both. Think of anything you have done recently, say in the past month or two, and see whether it fits under one of those categories. To get an idea of how much enjoyment and meaning these activities bring you, rate them on a 1 to 10 scale. If you include any enjoyable and meaningful activities you *used to do*, which you would like to bring back into your life, place a "P" next to those. Place an "F" next to any activity that creates flow for you.

After you build your lists, see if you notice any patterns. Is one column a lot more full than another? If your lists feel fairly empty or you see a number of low ratings, try not to get discouraged. Exploring your activity landscape is an important step all on its own, and I applaud you for it!

Later, we will be working on ways to add to your lists and boost your fuel levels. Just know that whatever you came up with has great potential to power your engine.

Now it's time to look at what's most important to you in life, tapping into the directional energy offered by your values and goals. This may lead you to think of some additional enjoyable and meaningful activities, which you could add to your list.

Steering Your Activities with Values

In his book *Man's Search for Meaning*, Victor Frankl (1962) wrote that a person who has a "why" in life can endure quite a bit of hardship, finding many ways to thrive in spite of it. For this reason, he suggested we shine a spotlight on what's most important to us. The clearer we are about our "why," the better we can direct our actions every day to fulfill these important life purposes.

You can think of your "why" in life as values, the principles that steer your activities. Miller, C'de Baca, and Matthews (2001) developed a publicly available list of eighty-three positive values you can read through to see what your best matches are. The list includes family, friendship, love, spirituality, fun, fitness, inner peace, and so many others. Almost anything that adds meaning to your week can count as a value. You will also notice that many of your values double as personal strengths.

The more you are aware of your values, the stronger your "why" becomes. As a result, you can get a better "grip" on your steering wheel. And the better you can steer, the more effectively you can meet your goals.

Let's pause here so that you can think about what your top values might be. You may not need to look at an extensive list to know what they are. Write down the first three or four values that come to mind. There's a good chance they are your top steering forces.

As we move forward, here are four key points to remember about values:

- **They can serve as directional guides for your actions.** A value of kindness, for example, can motivate you to help someone in need.

- **They can shape your short-term and long-term goals.** To satisfy your value of learning, you might set a long-term goal of completing a graduate degree. In the short-term, you might plan to read a book on a subject you want to study.

- **They can help you persevere through stressful circumstances.** The value of family might add fuel to an intensive job search if you are currently out of work. Faith, as another example, has guided many people through adversity.

- **They can contribute to your well-being and self-care when you align your activities with them.** You can feel especially good when your activities line up with what's most important to you. You are also caring for yourself whenever you take a step toward satisfying your purpose in life, whatever that may be.

As Frankl suggested, you can create enjoyment and meaning any time you are actively in touch with what matters most to you. This next exercise will guide you in creating direct connections between your values, goals, and activities. It can power up your VPS, or "Values Positioning System."

EXERCISE: Steering Your Values with Activities

For this exercise, you will want to take out the list of enjoyable and meaningful activities you created earlier and carve out about fifteen to twenty minutes of time. In building your VPS, you will be linking your values and goals to some of those activities. You will also be developing new activities that could fall under "enjoyable," "meaningful," or "both." If there's space on your list, you can use it, but you might want to have extra sheets of paper on hand.

Step 1—Linking Values and Activities: You can take two paths to connecting your values with activities.

> **Path 1:** Look at your activity columns and write down one or more personal values that each activity expresses or fulfills. For example, if you listed painting, you might jot down "creativity." For conversations with a relative, you might put down "family," "love," and "humor." Draw a line connecting each value with any other related activities across your columns.

> **Path 2:** Instead of moving from activities to values, you can move from values to activities. If you choose this path, you would start by developing a comprehensive values list. You can start with the three or four top personal values you previously identified and add others that fit from the online Personal Values Card Sort (Miller et al. 2001). Asking yourself, "Where do I want to be in five years?" and "What values are important in getting me there?" can help too.

> Once you are satisfied with your values list, write down, for *each value*, as many activities in your life as you can think of, past or present. For example, activities that fulfill the value of family could include dinners together, conversations, watching movies, and caring for an ill family member. Some activities may already be on your earlier list, but others may not. If they are not on the list, go ahead and add them.

Step 2—Building Out Your Connections: Are you satisfied with the number and frequency of activities tied to each of your most important values? If the answer is yes for all of them, great! You can move on to Step 3. If, however, you find that one or more values aren't getting the "activity attention" they deserve, answer the following questions:

- What other actions could I take to satisfy that value going forward?

- Do I want to give more time to a particular activity to better satisfy that value?

- Is there someone in my life who can help me meet my values more fully? A friend? Family member? Coworker?

Don't worry about how realistic the new activities you come up with seem. The aim right now is to collect all the possibilities. You can decide later where they might fit into your schedule.

Step 3—Linking Values and Activities to Goals: On a separate sheet of paper, list two short-term goals (what you want to accomplish within the next three months or so) and two long-term goals (what you want to accomplish six months from now or longer). Then look at your values-activity connections to see which of them are tied to these goals.

You might see, for example, that your short-term goal of running three miles after a surgery is connected to your value of fitness. The activities that will help you reach that goal include stretching, eating healthy foods, and running shorter distances as you work your way up toward that goal. Meeting a long-term goal of maintaining sobriety might depend on your active values of family connection, love, and spirituality. Activity-wise, this might involve spending time with a sponsor, attending family functions, and cultivating love through spiritual practice.

I recognize that this exercise is a bit more complicated than others, so good for you if you went through each step. Please take your time with it, and come back to it on different days if that makes it more manageable.

As you complete this exercise, you might be wondering, "What's the key takeaway?" The answer is a stronger center of meaning, motivation, and direction in life. A higher awareness of the connection between your values and your activities can reveal a clearer path toward what you want to accomplish.

For example, eating in healthy ways may become a top priority when you realize its link to your values of health and fitness. It may feel good just to see how *what you are doing right now* fulfills your values while advancing you toward your goals. As a result, these goals may seem more attainable, brightening your outlook on the future, no matter what stage of life you are in (Feldman, Rand, and Kahle-Wrobleski 2009).

That's what happened for Jonathan, a sixty-five-year-old artist, as he completed this exercise. He identified values of creativity, teaching, being a good provider, caring for the environment, and being a strong leader. His short-term goals centered around summer reading and creating a working photography studio, activities that were aligned with his deeper values of teaching and creativity. This exercise brought clarity to Jonathan's path in life. He planned to use his written list of values and goals in a daily meditation to further fuel his directions as an artist and educator.

Like Jonathan, you may feel an intensification of meaning and hope by working with your values. This is all part of making happiness more second nature. Establishing greater consistency between action and purpose moves you closer to your best possible self. It can also guide your overall goals around wellness, which we will explore next.

Bringing It Back to the Dimensions of Wellness

We have usually waited until the end of each week's journey to look at how positivity fits within the seven wellness areas. But since you have already done a considerable amount of work in thinking about your values-activity connections, let's see now how they can support your overall sense of well-being. As a reminder, our seven key wellness areas are relationships, physical health, leisure, creativity/knowledge, work, finances, and spirituality.

Using the list you made in the Steering Your Activities section, re-sort your activities under these seven categories. How much enjoyment and meaning do you find in each area? You may discover that you have a lot of values, activities, and goals that line up with one wellness area, like work. Enjoyment and meaning may abound there. You also may notice that you have fewer activities contributing to another area, such as physical health. For now, this is an "observation only" zone.

As you become more aware of your wellness activity landscape, here are three other important points about it:

- **We might naturally pour activity fuel into some wellness areas over others.** You don't *need* to balance out your fuel across the seven wellness domains, unless you feel particularly bothered by your levels. If, for example, spirituality is not something that's important to you, it would make sense for you to invest your energy in other areas.

- **Your activity levels may rise, fall, or change in focus over time.** It is normal for activity levels to vary in intensity and focus. For example, the summer months may lend themselves more to leisure, while the fall could center around work. A family crisis could cause you to shift your activity fuels into relationships. An injury or illness, on the other hand, could make you concentrate on physical health. Being compassionate toward yourself for these shifts, whether they are expected or not, is a *Happier You* must.

- **We need rest and should not underestimate its importance.** At times, your body and mind may ask for rest. Giving yourself permission to slow down can protect you against burnout. Low-activity periods, no matter where they fall, can help ensure you have enough energy to continue down the road toward your goals.

Keeping the flower philosophy in mind, if you do see a particular wellness area in your life that's calling out for some activity replenishment, try to look at this as an opportunity for growth rather than a frustrating deficit. For many of us, work and relationships stand out as places that could use more enjoyment fuel. The next exercise will offer some practice with this kind of activity tune-up.

EXERCISE: Activity Tune-Ups

Things we do every day can lose their luster. Usually, they involve a routine task, something we do repeatedly that has become tiresome or dull. In this exercise, we will build on the skills from Weeks 3 and 4 around transforming ordinary life. If you've already tried them out, great! It means you already have some practice deepening your appreciation of common activities and finding their lighter side. If not, this exercise will make an excellent starting point.

It offers five ways to tune up your enjoyment and meaning levels: activity pairing, ending with rewards, mining for meaning, creating space, and changing locations and times. The exercise will take about fifteen minutes to complete and will require some paper.

Let's first take a look at each of the tune-up methods. After you read through them, feel free to jump right into the exercise's two steps.

- **Activity Pairing:** With this approach, you place a more enjoyable activity alongside a less enjoyable one. For example, you might listen to your favorite upbeat song while cleaning. Or you might eat something you like while studying for an exam or responding to emails. Exercising with a friend versus doing it alone is another form of pairing, one that can also add pleasure and meaning.

- **Ending with Rewards:** Here, you would reward yourself with something you enjoy after you complete an activity. The reward could be a treat, time to relax, playing a game—really anything that brings you pleasure.

- **Mining for Meaning:** In this method, you would ask yourself, "What makes this meaningful to do?" or "What would be a good result from this?" For any kind of cleaning or organizing task, you might think about how calm you will likely feel once everything is neat. Or, if you're trying to change your diet to make it more nutritious, consider the health benefits that could inspire you to stick with it.

- **Creating Space:** One way to tune up less enjoyable or meaningful activities is to space them out. For example, instead of spending three hours straight on a report from work, you might spread it out across the day, perhaps in one-hour or thirty-minute blocks. In between, you could plan something more enjoyable or allow yourself to rest.

- **Changing Locations and Times:** You can make activities more enjoyable or meaningful if you move them to new locations, schedule them at different times, or both. The shift can be a small one. You might decide, for example, to read outdoors in the morning as opposed to reading in bed at night. Switching things up in this way can leave you feeling more alert or energized.

Now that you're familiar with the tune-up methods, it's time to apply one or more of them.

Step 1: Look at your list of activities from earlier and select one with low enjoyment or meaning ratings. Alternatively, you could choose from the list of everyday activities from Weeks 3 and 4. Another option is to make a new list of activities that feel like chores and pick one from there. Examples might include doing laundry or yard work, or answering emails.

Step 2: Apply one or more of the tune-up strategies from above to the activity the next time you do it. Afterward, ask yourself how it went. See if your ratings of enjoyment and meaning increased.

You might need to experiment with different tune-up approaches and see which is the best fit for that activity. For example, mining for meaning may work well for work-related tasks, but not as well for household chores.

Keeping tabs on your enjoyment and meaning levels will give you a sense of how good your fit is. You could also use the seven wellness areas to focus your activity-enhancement work, applying your new tune-up strategies to activities in one or more of those areas. Check out the "Activity Tune-Ups" worksheet at http://www.newharbinger.com/47858, if that's helpful.

Another point to be mindful of this week is that not *every* activity needs to have high levels of enjoyment and meaning. If you have some on the lower end of the scales, you can attempt to meet them with acceptance. No tune-up required!

Now let's have a look at how Alyson infused her everyday activities with more meaning and enjoyment, which could inspire your own tune-ups.

Alyson's Story: Adding Sparks into Activities

Alyson saw activity tune-ups as a way to increase a sense of well-being. Several activities seemed like good candidates: short walks, household chores, and studying.

She decided to focus on pairing strategies first, adding a mindfulness practice to her walks. This helped her feel calmer and more absorbed in nature. Alyson also paired listening to her favorite music with washing dishes, which made the time go by faster. She describes the immediate positive effects: "I almost forget that I'm working because I'm singing along, dancing, or thinking about the lyrics at the same time."

For studying, Alyson chose spacing and rewards approaches. She took short ten-minute study breaks, during which she stretched, listened to a song, or watched a video. Thanks to all of these efforts, Alyson noticed feeling more enthusiastic about these parts of her routine. She rated her enjoyment and meaning higher on each. In fact, housework and her walks jumped a full four points on those scales.

How did revitalizing activities go for you? I am thrilled that you are trying, learning what works for you and what doesn't.

If refueling existing activities did not boost your levels of enjoyment and meaning enough, you may need new activities for your engine. That's where we're headed next.

New Activities for Your Engine

New activities can be things you've never done before or activities you've stopped but would like to add back into your life. It can also be another version of an existing activity.

Maybe you are getting tired of the same routine on weekends and want to add a morning hike. You may see an opportunity to strengthen your spiritual practice by getting involved with new faith-based activities. If meal times seem uninspired, you might try new recipes from cookbooks and social media feeds.

If you're in need of some ideas for new activities, your values and goals could be good starting points. For example, if you like adventure, you could ask yourself, "In what ways can I bring more adventure into my life?" The answers may be traveling places you've never been, trying new cuisines, or visiting an amusement park. If you have a goal of making work more fulfilling, your activity plan could include taking workshops around a topic of interest or developing projects in an area that excites you.

New activities do not need to be complicated. They can be as simple as singing along to a song you like or playing a board game you haven't played since you were a child. Maybe take a look at the list of activities here to see if any catch your eye:

Call a friend

Text a friend

Play a board game

Cook your favorite dish or meal

Go out of your house, even if just to sit outside

Join a group at your place of worship

Join a club

Write a letter to a friend

Write a letter to yourself

Take photos

Paint your nails

Call a family member you haven't spoken to in a long time

Give your pet a bath

Go for a long walk

Do yoga, tai chi, or Pilates

Lift weights

Stretch your muscles

Make something

Sing along to a song

Go outside and watch the birds

Go hiking

Do a puzzle with a lot of pieces

Change your hair color

Contribute to a good cause

Read your favorite book, magazine, newspaper, or poem

Watch a movie you haven't seen

Ask Alexa a question

Play a card game

Take a bike ride

Watch a funny movie

Listen to upbeat or calming music

Take a bubble bath or shower

Draw or paint a picture

Work in a garden

Sell something you don't want on the Internet

Take a nap

Take a class

Once you find a few new activities to add to your routines, the next step is scheduling them. It's a good idea to have some that are doable in shorter time frames, and some in longer. To begin your scheduling, what times of day or days of the week might offer windows? Being realistic is important. Are you more comfortable aiming for one new activity a week, or would you like to try for more than that?

To increase your sense of control over how you feel, you might take "rapid ratings" of enjoyment and meaning before, during, and immediately after each new activity you try. These ratings can guide you in making any necessary adjustments.

Some activities may give you more enjoyment, meaning, and flow when you do them alone. You may be more likely to enter a mindful state, and as a result, more deeply appreciate the thoughts, feelings, and sensations that go along with that activity. For example, it could be easier to enjoy nature when you ride a bike alone.

You might find that you prefer being social for some activities. Shopping, eating, running, and traveling might fall into this category. Even traditionally solitary activities like reading, drawing, writing, and painting can have a social side. Enjoyment and meaning can come through sharing what you create or experience. A sense of connection, caring, love, and understanding may peak in this gear.

You can also experiment to see how engaging in your activities alone, and then with someone else, might intensify their positive effects. This next exercise will help you do just that, highlighting the social and solitary sides of your activities. In a tangible way, from a child's mind perspective, it will also ask you to honor the ways in which stillness and activity support your well-being.

EXERCISE: Child's Mind—Activities in Two Gears

Stillness and activity are essential parts of being whole. We are often happiest when we have balance between these states. In the spirit of honoring this balance, identify something in your life that represents you in a state of motion and something else that represents you in stillness. For motion, some possibilities include a bicycle, ball, running sneaker, or photograph of you doing something active. Objects that capture stillness could include a blanket, book, pillow, or peaceful song.

Every time this week that you make contact with these objects, think about the values of calmness or being in motion, depending on what the object represents. For example, when you use your favorite blanket on the sofa, you might think, *Settling into a quiet and relaxed place recharges me.* When you ride a bicycle, your thought might be, *My body thanks me for being in motion.* Notice any positive emotion signposts that follow.

This next part of the exercise is meant to help you find a stronger appreciation for activities you do by yourself and those you do with others. You could consider these your solitary and social activity "gears." You will want to try out *both* gears, noticing the pleasure and meaning fuel levels for each.

The idea is fairly simple. Over the next week, pick one activity you would like to do alone and one that you would like to do with others. It actually could be the same activity, if you want. For example, you could have lunch alone one day and plan a dinner with others for later in the week. Follow these steps during the activities, or afterward:

Step 1: Identify the value or values the activity fulfills.

Step 2: Notice whether there was a stillness or motion to the activity. You may have experienced some of both. What did you like most about the stillness? Or what kind of energy came from being in motion? Was it physical, emotional, or spiritual?

Step 3: Measure your overall enjoyment and meaning levels from being in each gear, on a 1 to 10 scale. What was the best part of being by yourself? How about with others? Which of the sixteen positive emotion signposts did you notice?

Step 4: Take stock of how much control and hope you felt after being in your social and solitary gears. Could you move easily between them, or was it difficult? Do you want to practice shifting into one gear more often over the next week or so?

By honoring yourself in motion and stillness, with others and by yourself, you are strengthening self-acceptance. It is perfectly fine if you prefer one gear over another. Some of us enjoy alone time more than socializing, or being in motion more than stillness. Whatever you discover about yourself during this exercise, I invite you to consider it a rousing success!

Reflection Point

This week you have explored how activities can energize your life and bring you closer to what's most important to you. You have likely seen how adding new activities or reshaping old ones can heighten the pleasure of each day, deepen life's meaning, and build hope for the future.

How did it go for you? Try to honor any experience you had with your activity-sculpting. As a reminder, you can stop and start your movement through this book any time you want!

To review, this week's four Core Positivity Practices are:

- Seeing the enjoyment and meaning in what you do every day
- Aligning activities with your values and goals
- Making activities more enjoyable or meaningful
- Connecting activities in your life with multiple areas of wellness

The menu of exercises around these areas consists of:

- Your Positive Activity Chains
- Connecting Your Activities with Values
- Activity Tune-ups
- Child's Mind—Activities in Two Gears

This week, you also identified "switch flippers" to build positive-activity momentum, and worked to clarify which activities provided the most enjoyment and meaning. Looking back over your efforts, I hope you see that you've covered a lot of ground!

Before we step into the realm of kindness in the next week, I wonder if you could take a moment, close your eyes, and appreciate *all* of what you do as a whole. See if you can honor your unique combination of activities, directions, and speeds.

There is a wonder in how our engines propel us forward and an excitement in the possibilities they open up. With your movements, big and small, you determine your sense of meaning and enjoyment each day. You are continuing to build resilience that way, as purpose and pleasure help you keep any obstacles you face in the proper perspective.

A Gentle Smile
Revealing the Springs of Kindness

The fragrance always stays in the hand that gives the rose. —Hada Bejar

There is a story that shows how important kindness is to our personal well-being, and to the well-being of humankind.

During a celebration of the growing season, a nine-year-old boy named Siddhartha Gautama watched the fields being ploughed for the first time. He noticed the tremendous strain placed on the buffalo pulling the plough. He felt the difficulty of the field worker who labored under the hot noon sun. He felt sad for the worms churned up by the plough, and for a small bird snapped up by a hawk while feeding on the worms.

As he watched these events unfold, Siddhartha realized the interconnected nature of all living things. He understood, then, that no matter what our conditions in life, all living creatures want to avoid suffering and feel at peace (Gutsol 2019). The awareness of a closely connected world led Siddhartha to feel great compassion for everything around him, a key part of his journey toward becoming the Buddha, which means "Enlightened One."

Kindness springs from this kind of deep caring. It flows from understanding that we live as an interconnected global community, and that we all have great worth by simply being alive. Our collective happiness relies, in large part, on how we treat each other. It rests in what we give in words and actions to those we know and to those we don't. It is an essential part of caring for ourselves, which in turn helps sustain the world.

Whether we are encouraging a friend, paying a coworker a compliment, or volunteering to help those less fortunate, kindness confirms the bonds we share. What's more, as fellow travelers facing common difficulties in life, like heartbreak, loss, and illness, we all *deserve* to receive kindness.

As we near the last part of this seven-week program, being kind to yourself and to others can help you continue along the positive path you're on. It can support all your *Happier You* efforts to live with more resilience, strength, and happiness.

Here are some key points about kindness to keep in mind:

- **Kindness is not complicated.** Being kind is not a complex skill. You likely give to others in your life in many ways already, some of which may seem very small, such as with compliments or providing help with a chore.

- **Kindness makes us feel good.** Not only do we get pleasure from being nice to others and to ourselves, but it also reduces negative feelings (Binfet and Whitehead 2019). If you are kind, you may enjoy a stronger sense of purpose in life, better physical health, and greater self-acceptance (Schwartz et al. 2009).

- **Kindness flows from empathy.** We are more likely to be kind to someone if we can put ourselves in their shoes (Beechler 2018), like Siddhartha did during the ploughing festival. If we can imagine others' struggles as if they were our own, we are more likely to help them.

- **Kindness connects us to others.** When we are kind to people in our lives, we often feel closer to them and they feel closer to us (Aspy and Proeve 2017).

- **Kindness can be a guiding value.** People value kindness to different degrees. If we make kindness a priority, it can shape our actions, words, and thoughts in positive ways.

As you keep these ideas in mind, we'll begin by spotting the presence of kindness and examining the inner sources from which it flows.

Where Kindness Comes From

You may already see yourself as a kind person, which is great! But have you ever wondered why that is the case? What makes you a kind person? Where do you think your kindness comes from?

It could be part of how you were raised, taught to you by parents, teachers, or friends. It could also come from your values or spiritual practice. Many religions emphasize it, including Christianity, Hinduism, and Buddhism. You could practice kindness simply because it feels good and brings you closer to important people in your life.

It is also true that you may not be in touch with kindness as much as you would like. Good-heartedness can be especially challenging when life is hard, if something painful has happened to you, or if you suffer from chronic illness, depression, or anxiety.

In this week's work, we will spend some time focusing on how to unblock the kindness instinct, if you do feel stuck. Getting more familiar with where your good-heartedness comes from (or where it *could* come from) is a key to increasing its positive footprint in your life. Let's begin by looking at a variety of kindness sources.

Six Sources of Kindness

It is easier to be kind when we feel good within ourselves. Here are six ways of sparking those positive feelings, each of which can create a solid foundation for good-heartedness:

- **Finding physical calm.** Pleasant sensations can help you relax, such as a warm bath, essential oils, massage, or deep breathing. A calm physical state can also follow a good night's rest, vigorous workout, or nutritious meal.

- **Visualizing or visiting a place of tranquility.** You can close your eyes and picture yourself at a beach, forest, or anywhere else that is peaceful—real or imagined. Actually going there is another way to get in touch with a sense of peace.

- **Returning to gratitude.** Thinking of what gifts are in your life now, in this moment, can replenish your emotional reserves and invite contentment. When we feel content, it is easier to give of ourselves.

- **Creating enjoyable and meaningful "me" time.** Scheduling enjoyable or meaningful activities you identified in Week 5 can lower frustration and fill your kindness reservoir. Anything that gives you a break from stress counts. It could be setting aside time for your favorite hobby, working in a garden, going shopping, taking walks, or reading that book you've been wanting to read.

- **Reaching for something transcendent.** You might turn to spiritual practice, which could include prayer, meditation, connecting with nature, or conversing with your higher power. In reaching for these heights, you might be filled with a profound feeling of universal kindness.

- **Spending time with someone who is kind.** Do you know someone who is often kind? If so, see if you can plan a time to talk with them or be in their presence. Just making contact with this person in your life can create a feeling of ease, and their kindness could soak into you.

I would invite you to pick three of your strongest sources from this list, or from any personal sources not included here. Take that warm bath. Visualize yourself on the beach. Call your friend who always has something nice to say.

After you do, take a moment to see where it carries you, emotionally, physically, socially, and spiritually. You will want to observe how that source affects your desire to be kind. How good-hearted do you feel afterward, on a scale of 1 to 10? Is that different from how you felt before you accessed that source?

I hope you see that when we are kind to ourselves in these ways, we increase how much we have to give others. Filling your cup like this not only feels good, it also allows you to pour from it into the world. Nikki offers us a wonderful description of this inside-out connection.

Nikki's Story: Drawing from the Springs

Nikki is an ever-curious thirty-three-year-old who radiates kindness. She prioritizes family, friends, a growth mindset, and gratitude in her daily Happier You practice, all of which are connected to her kindness sources.

In reflecting on those sources, Nikki found that feeling rested, grateful, socially connected, and transcendent brought out her kindest self. For example, she described how surrounding herself with considerate people led to a kindness "ripple effect," where everyone helped prepare and clean up after a dinner. That feeling of togetherness opened the gate to good-heartedness for her even further.

She wrote, "I am often in awe of how connected we all truly are—in a beautiful dance with nature. I start to think of the world around me and the impact that I can have. It seems like only a natural decision to feed more kindness into the world. So I choose to live kindness by offering kind thoughts to others, by recycling, by saying a prayer, by taking time to appreciate the beauty of nature."

Nikki realized that feeling lonely can become a source of kindness too. In those moments, she often sends a text to a friend, sharing something she loves about them. The connection created by this small act of kindness makes the loneliness fade. She also feels inspired to express kindness simply by hearing about the kindness of others, showing just how far the ripples can travel.

Spotting Kindness

Now that you have worked a bit with inner sources, let's work on becoming a better kindness-spotter.

Can you recall a time in the past week when you helped someone else, or when someone helped you? It could have been something small, like talking on the phone to a friend or doing extra work around the house. Notice what thoughts or feelings arise for you as you stream that moment. Did you feel closer to that person, calmer, or less affected by stress? Which of the sixteen signposts came up? Perhaps those feelings included love, compassion, connectedness, and joy.

Deep-dive questions like this can help reveal and replenish your inner springs of kindness, following A Happier You's inside-out approach to well-being. As you have likely already found through this program, cultivating positive emotions and thoughts makes it more likely you will send that positivity outward. Kindness is no different. The happier you feel, the easier it is to be kind to others (North, Tarrant, and Hargreaves 2004).

The positive effects of kindness can flow back into you as well. Being kind to others can improve your mood (Rowland and Curry 2019). In fact, the more kind acts you do, the happier you can feel. Interestingly, Rowland and Curry found these positive effects were equally strong no matter how close people felt to each other. Kindness is powerful when directed toward family and acquaintances alike.

Let's now take a look at the varieties of kindness and where they already come through in your life.

Kindness in Words, Thoughts, and Actions

Kindness takes on many forms, just as water coming up from the earth can take many paths. You can channel it through your words, thoughts, and actions. While we commonly think of kindness as an action, something we *do*, we can also express it powerfully in what we *say*. You can acknowledge someone's strengths, point out something nice they did, provide encouragement during a tough time, or ask if there's some way you can be helpful.

Kindness does not need words to flow. A soft tone in your voice, smiling, nodding, leaning in, and making eye contact all convey respect and care in a conversation. It expresses an attitude of patience, gentleness, and putting others first. Great teachers in our lives often show these qualities.

Kind actions do not have to be big actions, or cost much. They can include doing small favors for friends or coworkers, helping a family member with chores, holding a door open for someone, and posting positive messages on social media. These kind gestures can easily spread. For example, paying for someone's coffee can inspire that person to do the same for someone else.

In addition to its expression through actions and language, kindness can emerge in how you *think* about yourself, others, and the world around you. Kind thoughts in these areas are likely to become visible actions. The thought *I deserve a break* can blossom into making space for your self-care. Thinking *She was considerate in offering me help* could lead you to offer help in return. The thought *I hope everyone affected by the storm is okay* can prompt donating to those affected.

Kindness stimulates these positive thinking-doing-feeling pathways. It's an example of the same "upward spirals" you have been learning to intentionally create across all the positivity skill areas of *A Happier You*.

As you become more thoughtful about kindness, consider these questions to help shape your approach:

- If I were going to show kindness, would it be through words, actions, or thoughts?

- Do I have a preferred pathway?

- Is there someone in my life I would like to direct more kindness toward? If so, through which channel?

In answering these questions, you have begun to develop a kindness plan for the week. By the way, it's fine if the focus of your plan is you! We'll look at that more carefully later. But first, I'd like to share an exercise that can sharpen your ability to see where kindness already touches your life in words, thoughts, and actions.

EXERCISE: Three of a Kind

Throughout *A Happier You*, you have practiced streaming and spotlighting the best parts of who you are, what you do, and what happens to you. Here we'll apply these skills to kindness. You will first look for examples of receiving kindness and then move into a search for your giving moments. Ready to begin?

Step 1: To narrow down your streaming window, you could pick the last week or two, or even just the past couple days. Since small kindnesses often fly under the radar, the better recollection you have, the easier it will be to identify them. A recent streaming window can help with that. Alternatively, if you feel you haven't been the recipient of much kindness lately, you can pick a larger time range, say the past year or more, and look for lighthouses of kindness—those brighter examples that stand out in your memory. Kindness lighthouses could include a friend helping you move, unexpectedly receiving a heartfelt letter, or someone at work stepping in to assist you in a major way.

Step 2: As you stream a chosen period of time, make a list of any and all kind words, actions, body language, or overall attitudes directed *toward you*—as many as you can remember. The smallest compliments, tiny helpful acts, and any bits of thoughtfulness count! If you can, see if you can identify at least one example in each of our three main categories: words, actions, and body language. Don't worry, however, if one or more categories remains empty. As long as you recorded something, you can move on to Step 3.

Step 3: Pick one or two examples of kindness to spotlight from your list. Ask yourself some or all of the following deep-dive questions:

- What does it mean about me that I received this kindness?
- Which of the positive sixteen signposts went along with it?
- What positive effects did that kindness have on the rest of my day or week?
- How did it affect my readiness to return kindness in some way?
- How might my relationships benefit from it?

Step 4: Now repeat Steps 1 to 3 for any kind acts you've displayed *toward others*, and ask yourself these slightly modified deep-dive questions:

- What does it mean about me that I expressed kindness in this way?
- What positive emotion signposts appeared for both me and the recipient?
- How did that act strengthen our relationship?
- Did showing kindness in this way help me better handle stress? If so, how?

This exercise may offer positive insights into yourself. You might learn, for example, that you have a much deeper kindness reservoir than you had originally thought. Seeing the effects of all the ways you give to others may boost your sense of well-being and resilience. It may also stimulate fresh ideas about how you would like to show kindness.

One final way to use this exercise is repeating Step 4 with kind thoughts. You might want to narrow your stream to the past day or even the past couple hours, since thoughts flow quickly through the mind and are easily forgotten.

.   You could search your mental stream for any time you wished someone well, felt the desire to lend a hand, or admired someone's strength. Perhaps the best deep-dive question related to thought-streaming is, "In what ways did these thoughts lift me up?" You might also consider whether each thought might translate into actions or words.

While this streaming exercise involves looking back, you can also set a kindness intention for the week ahead and watch for moments that emerge in these three areas. This is how Kevin approached his kindness-catching.

Kevin's Story: Kindness-Catching

Kevin began his week with an intention to be kind in words, actions, and thoughts. One opportunity arose in his job as a supervisor. He allowed good-heartedness to guide a conversation with a team member who was struggling to balance her responsibilities. He pointed out her strengths on the job, namely her teamwork, work ethic, and passion for her role. Kevin also expressed confidence in her leadership skills. She left that meeting feeling supported, connected, and inspired.

Kevin also decided to express kindness through writing, exchanging letters with his aunt and a friend he has known for twenty years. Kind thoughts and actions again came together for him as he planned to provide some financial help to a friend who had lost his father while in college.

As a result of keeping his spotlight on kindness during the week, Kevin described feeling more rooted in the present moment and less anxious about the future. The saying "Kindness is never wasted" came to mind, a message he shared with another friend, in hopes that it would inspire him in similar ways.

Obstacles to Kindness

Kindness may not always *feel* accessible, and for understandable reasons. Our kindness instinct may be blocked by problems at work or home, conflict in relationships, strain on finances, poor health, a stressful day, painful memories that resurface, or perceived slights from others. If you ordinarily give much of yourself to others, you might also suffer from "kindness exhaustion." Thoughts like *I have nothing left in me to give today* or feelings of frustration might spill over into your daily life. Kindness blockages can also arise from not having your basic needs met, which include safety, belonging, love, and nourishment.

The question is, what can we do about these obstacles? If the problem involves basic needs that aren't being met at the moment, the answer could be to plan acts of self-kindness. This next exercise offers some additional strategies to help you open kindness channels and meet your barriers with both compassion and creativity.

EXERCISE: Helping Kindness Flow

In this exercise, you will explore ways you can set the stage for kindness. It has three parts, which you may want to spread out over a few days: 1) identifying flow-encouragers, 2) understanding flow-stoppers, and 3) showing yourself kindness. You will want to have a notebook handy for each part, so you can keep a record of your insights.

Part 1: Identifying Flow-Encouragers

In the first part of this exercise, I invite you to think about what makes kindness easier to channel for you. I call these your "flow-encouragers." You may discover, for example, that you are kinder when you have chances to spend time with friends or focus on self-care, which can include getting enough sleep and exercise. Perhaps kindness rushes forth when you feel happy about a good event in your life, like getting engaged or receiving a job offer.

You might find that just thinking about your value of kindness, even in the face of personally stressful circumstances, opens the gates to it.

Asking yourself these questions can help you identify your flow-encouragers:

- What thoughts or feelings increase the probability I will show kindness toward others?

- When do I have the greatest tendency to show kindness?

- Who or what in my life inspires kindness?

- Did something that happened to me in the past make me want to express kindness? If so, what was it?

Let's pause here to dive deeper into the sources that these questions revealed. See if you can think of an interaction with someone, or an event in your life, that gave rise to kindness. Bring it to mind as vividly as possible, so you can catch all the thoughts, feelings, actions, and words around that kindness.

I would encourage you to write down what you catch, so you can stay in close contact with these flow-encouragers in the days ahead. Our goal right now is simply gaining a better awareness of where to find our kindest states of mind. That being said, if you feel inspired to say or do something nice for someone right now, fantastic!

Part 2: Understanding Flow-Stoppers

The next part of this exercise involves taking a closer look at your kindness flow-stoppers. These questions can help you do that:

- Where and when do I feel most blocked from showing my kind self?

- What feelings interfere the most? Anger? Frustration? Sadness?

- Do I feel that past hurts need to heal before I'll be able to open that gate more fully?

- Am I blocked by a lack of emotional, physical, social, or spiritual sustenance?

Remember that a greater awareness is all we're looking for right now; however, if your answers spark a plan to get the springs flowing again, that's great! Maybe the solution is spending less time around someone who is negative, or starting therapy during a challenging time in your life. Perhaps you see value in returning to the work of an earlier week in this program, like gratitude or humor.

Just knowing what stands in your path could lead to subtle positive changes in how you interact with others and how you treat yourself. I encourage you to write down one or two flow-stoppers and what you might do to address them.

Part 3: Showing Yourself Kindness

If you recall, we started our *Happier You* work in Week 1 talking about the meadow of acceptance, that place of quiet, nonjudgmental observation. If you are hurting in some way, stepping into that meadow can be the first movement toward encouraging kindness to flow again. This is what we will focus on now.

To start, you want to make sure you have an especially compassionate mindset. If you find you can't stop your critical self-talk or you feel flooded by negative thoughts, you might want to wait until that commentary quiets down. Or you could try Step 1 and see how it goes, stopping if you feel too much resistance.

I should also add: if you're feeling good right now and you don't have any barriers to kindness that you want to address, you could review these steps to know what to do if or when you *do* encounter a flow-stopper. Ready to get started?

Step 1: Offer yourself a gift of self-compassion in the form of a thought or statement. Examples are *I see that I'm upset and in pain, so I'm going to embrace myself with gentleness until it passes,* or *It's okay to feel blocked from kindness because of how I've been hurt in the past. I understand why I feel this way.* Any gesture of self-compassion would fit well here. You could also call to mind the idea that everyone feels pain and you are not alone in your struggle. This awareness of our "common humanity" (Neff 2003) can be soothing.

Step 2: Now imagine surrounding the difficulty inside you with warmth, safety, and calm. Perhaps picture the still waters of a pond filling in around it. If this hurt rests in the distant past, you could visualize yourself as you are today, your wisest self, sitting beside this more vulnerable self. Put your arm around the more vulnerable version of yourself and offer some words of hope and comfort, like *It will be okay* and *I'm here for you.*

Step 3: Recognize that you are more than your suffering and deserve to feel better. Here you are acknowledging your essential worth and dignity. A thought like *Because I exist, I am deserving of peace* says that you are worthwhile *no matter what.* There are likely many other reasons you are worth kindness too, such as being a hard worker, good parent, loving son or daughter, or community advocate. Writing down some of those reasons can serve as a good reminder of *why* you would like to be kind to yourself, which is just as important as the *how.*

Step 4: Choose to do something kind for yourself now. You might nurture yourself by going for a walk, getting a massage, preparing a favorite meal, or anything else that might bring you comfort or enjoyment.

You can try these steps of self-kindness in a different order, or select one or two that ring the truest for you. It is perfectly okay if you need more time with any step. Turning the meadow of acceptance into a meadow of self-compassion can take some time. Coming back to it later is always an option too. Check out the "Practicing Self-Kindness" worksheet at http://www.newharbinger.com/47858, if that's helpful.

I want to applaud you for your kindness exploration so far. You have looked at conditions that bring kindness to the surface and those that may keep it from appearing. You may already have some ideas about how to unblock yourself, and even have taken steps toward surrounding yourself with compassion. You can "test the waters" of your work so far by asking, "How ready am I now to direct kindness outward?" and giving a rating on our familiar 1 to 10 scale.

Empathy as a Path to Kindness

Empathy is another kindness-enhancing skill, one that deserves special attention. Empathy is our ability to understand what someone else is thinking and feeling, and usually involves conveying that understanding in some way. It is often kindled by the recognition of our shared humanity. The better we can imagine what others go through, the more likely we will want to extend kindness to them (Beechler 2018).

For example, it is common to empathize with someone's struggle. If you see someone going through the loss of a loved one, you might put yourself in their place and look at their experience as if it were happening to you. Your empathy might include thoughts like *That must be extremely painful. They'll need someone to help them through it.*

Relating in this way can deepen the desire to be kind. In fact, the more accurately you can "feel your way into" another's world like this, the more good-heartedness can emerge.

Like our other forms of positivity in this program, empathy can be learned and strengthened. Here are a couple ways to do that:

- Ask someone you know to tell you about a stressful time. Instead of offering advice or an opinion, see if you can only use "reflective" statements like "It sounds like you felt…"; "That must have been…"; and "I can see how that affected you by…"

- Challenge yourself to extend empathy to others at random points throughout the week, verbally or in your thoughts. You don't have to know the person to guess what they might be thinking and feeling. You could prompt yourself with the questions, "If it were me in that situation, how might I react? What would I think or feel?"

You might choose to extend empathy toward yourself, as you have done any time you've stepped into the meadow of acceptance. It's worth spending a little extra time on this point since it is so important to our kindness instinct. Would you like to try a brief self-directed empathy practice now?

If so, think of a time you made a mistake that resulted in a fairly large problem. Maybe you said the wrong thing at work, angering a coworker, or you forgot a friend's birthday. Now imagine a close friend had made the same mistake. What would you tell them?

With forgetting the birthday, you might say, "I can see how awful you feel for having forgotten. I also can see that you are a good person and that you care about other people's feelings." For the coworker situation, you might say, "You had good intentions. Sometimes our words don't always come out right."

Why imagine your close friend as the empathy recipient? The reason is simple. Often it is easier to show others empathy than ourselves, particularly if we are highly self-critical. The last step, then, in this practice is to *tell yourself* what you would have told your friend. In other words, you become both the source *and* the recipient of empathy. The more you show *yourself* understanding, the easier it is to extend empathy to others.

As you practice empathy, I invite you to continue checking in on your desire to be kind. As a result of putting yourself in others' shoes, do you feel an urge to help others more often? Do you feel more closely connected to people in your life and in your community? I would not be at all surprised if the answer to both questions was yes.

While empathy paves a thoughtful, reflective path for acts of kindness, sometimes the most powerful types of kindness take us by surprise. We return now to child's mind to understand the delight that unexpected kindness can ignite.

EXERCISE: Child's Mind—The Surprises of Kindness

I'd like you to think back to a time in your childhood when you received a gift you had no idea was coming. Maybe it was praise for a school assignment, a birthday present from a relative, or an unplanned afternoon of fun on a family outing. If you look for signposts, I'm guessing joy would be among them. The fact that it was a surprise probably made it all the more delightful.

As we see in those examples, kindness can have an enormous effect on positivity when it is given and received unexpectedly. This exercise will allow you to deliver surprise expressions of kindness to one or more people in your life. It's similar to the child's mind exercise in Week 3 that asked you to create "Grati-Notes," messages of thankfulness written on sticky notes that you put in places where others would stumble upon them.

In this version of the exercise, you would do the same thing. These notes, however, will entirely focus on the recipient by:

- Pointing out a strength or positive quality in that person

- Sharing an inspirational message you think they could benefit from

- Describing an act of kindness you will do for that person upon discovery of the note

Your goal is to hide the notes in places where they will not be found right away, adding to the sense of excitement upon discovery. Similar to the Grati-Notes exercise, you can set up a kindness exchange, where you take turns creating and hiding notes for each other. The whole family could participate, with each family member assigned a different-color sticky note.

You could do it with coworkers or leave notes of general kindness in public places, creating unseen ripple effects of good-heartedness.

Take notice of all the good effects this activity has on your relationships and your emotional well-being. You may find that it makes kindness a higher priority in your life. You may also find that your conversations are more positive and you feel closer to those you care about. In many ways, you can think of these kindness notes as small springs of resilience. No matter what is happening in your life, kindness hands you the power to make yourself and others happier.

Your Kindness Plan

I am excited that you have devoted your energy to thinking about kindness and its sources this week! One way you can work with these insights is by creating a kindness plan, so you can practice kindness regularly and track the effects it has in your life. How does that sound to you?

Like Kevin's story from earlier, your plan can be a general one. You could hold the intention to be kind in thoughts, actions, and words, and see where that leads you. On the other hand, you could add specifics—the who, what, when, and where—if that feels right for you.

For example, you could plan to get in touch with kindness once in the morning, afternoon, and evening, letting the form and direction be spontaneous. You might offer a kind word to someone in the morning, be kind to yourself by carving out time to exercise in the afternoon, and lend an empathetic ear to a friend at the end of the day.

Another plan could involve showing kindness to a particular person in your life: a parent, child, teacher, coworker, friend, or someone who you don't know well. You could surprise them with a kind note, as in the child's mind exercise, or set a goal of doing one nice thing for them each day.

Whatever your plan is, making it flexible is key! At the end of each day, see if you can set aside five to ten minutes to stream any moments of kindness that occurred. You could start that stream by asking yourself,

"How was kindness present in my life today?" You might then benefit from spotlighting those moments with questions like "What did I do to encourage it?" "Which of the sixteen signposts emerged?" and "How did it change my day?" Making some notes in your positivity catcher can allow you to look back on these gifts during more challenging times.

Reflection Point

This week you have cared for yourself and others through kindness. Remember that *any* small step toward good-heartedness can have far-reaching positive effects for you and others. My hunch is that simply reading this chapter has helped your kindness springs flow more freely. As a check-in, what is your kindness instinct telling you to do right now?

Your Core Positivity Practices for this week are:

- Catching examples of kindness in your life stream and noticing their effects

- Activating one or more of the six kindness sources

- Identifying flow-encouragers and flow-stoppers

- Showing self-kindness

- Strengthening empathy as a way of sparking kindness toward others

- Making a kindness plan

Here is a brief reminder of the exercises that are available to you:

- Three of a Kind

- Helping Kindness Flow

- Child's Mind—The Surprises of Kindness

With fewer exercises to choose from this week, I would encourage you to sprinkle in some of the other practices. Perhaps you'll want to sharpen your empathy skills by practicing reflective listening with others. You might intentionally activate a different kindness source each day, or develop a kindness plan that keeps you on track. Your plan could include setting aside some time in the evening to stream and spotlight any kindness given or received that day.

You certainly only want to do what feels manageable. Remember that being kind to yourself strengthens your foundation for outward kindness. There is a circulation of kindness in the world that is not always easy to see. But you can strengthen its flow through how you treat yourself and others every day. Whenever you feel that gentle smile rising from within, the world around you is smiling too.

The Embrace
Expanding the Boundaries of Love

Nobody has ever measured, not even poets, how much the heart can hold. —Zelda Fitzgerald

Affection. Fondness. Deep caring. Tenderness. Acceptance. Love is a force composed of all of these elements. It is an essential part of nature and humanity. In its purest form, love brings us closer to others: parents, children, friends, coworkers, even strangers.

When we express it without expecting anything in return, it opens the door to the deepest form of connectedness. Caring for an elder who is sick, comforting a child, or lending a hand to those in need are all examples of how love shines through our lives with its selflessness. It is how we are held together, as families and communities. It lives in all the beautiful things that we create, like artwork and skyscrapers. It drives our actions as teachers, parents, sons, daughters, siblings, and neighbors.

None of us would be here without love, and because we are here together in this world, we need it in order to thrive. It is not only a powerful part of well-being and positivity, but it is as fundamental to life as air, food, and water.

This final week of *A Happier You* is all about awakening the love within you, as a way of caring for yourself and those around you. In many ways, we have been talking about love all along. It is the current that flows beneath gratitude, laughter, enjoyment, kindness, personal strengths, and accomplishments.

I believe we all have the capacity to feel and express love. Sometimes we don't use that part of ourselves regularly, or it goes quiet as a result of difficult experiences in life. Does that ring true for you? If so, love may just need stronger and more consistent invitations to appear.

In the *Happier You* way, you can practice loving just as you would practice any other positivity skill, like gratitude or spotlighting positive moments. If you like, we can activate this essential positivity force right now.

Getting in Touch with Love

I invite you to close your eyes and think of someone you love deeply, either now or in the past. Bring to mind a time you may have received a welcome embrace from them. This embrace could be physical, or suggested by that person's delight in seeing you. How do you feel physically and emotionally in that embrace? Do any of the sixteen signposts arise? What thoughts are filling your mind?

This kind of welcome embrace can bring out feelings of contentment, peace, safety, and warmth. You may have thoughts like *I am loved* or *I can love others* that lift you up in enduring ways. As you stream that embrace, stay in it as long as you like. It is one more example of how you can extend the glowing reach of the best parts of who you are.

As the embrace streaming exercise shows, love can flow through physical contact like hugs and holding hands. But it's not limited to that. Your heart's embrace can also include pets, objects of great significance like an old family photograph, a cause that improves the human condition like fighting hunger, or your most enjoyable and meaningful activities from Week 5. Love can exist at the surface of life, or deep beneath what we say, do, and think. It can take on many forms, including creativity, fellowship, and spirituality.

The famous nineteenth-century poet Elizabeth Browning captured this truth when she wrote, "How do I love thee? Let me count the ways."

Of course, love is not always a positive experience. It can certainly cause pain when it is absent or when it is not reciprocated. But here, in the spirit of A Happier You, we will focus on its most positive elements. We will look at the ways in which it inspires hope, puts us at ease during stressful times, and connects us with others. And by focusing on love's positive dimensions, we will continue to build the strength that is necessary to endure times that are not so positive.

This week's exercises will concentrate on expanding love's boundaries, both within yourself and outside of yourself. My hope is that you will begin to see love emanating from everything you have done so far in this program, as well as from new, unexplored places in your life.

The first exercise is designed to help you better appreciate love's range and its positive effects in your life. We will begin by identifying the people, places, things, and activities through which love speaks—your affections. I like to think of affection as a force that draws you toward something or someone. It does not just mean physical attraction. Affection can touch every part of life—which is why it can be useful to create a map of it.

EXERCISE: Your Affections Map

This map will allow you to focus your spotlight on places where love is already strong in your life, such as with family or a partner. It can also reveal new pathways of affection you might like to forge, or existing ones you'd like to extend, perhaps around friendships or hobbies.

The exercise will take about ten to fifteen minutes and you'll need some paper to write down your reflections. As with our other exercises, a quiet spot and some uninterrupted time can support you in focusing.

Step 1: On a sheet of paper, create five columns, labeling each at the top with a different category of affection: People/Pets, Things,

Places, Activities, and Thoughts. In each category, list as many sources of love as you can think of. You will know if someone or something belongs on your list if they bring out your affection, a sense of being drawn toward them and feeling important or uplifted in their presence.

For example, you might feel love through spending time with a best friend, playing an instrument, visiting the beach, or holding a graduation photo in your hands. Remember that *you* and anything about yourself can be a source as well, such as a positive trait like caring deeply for others or being adventurous.

Once you have created your lists, rate the average strength of each affection "spark" on a scale of 1 to 100. This will help you understand the scope and intensity of your love across many areas of life.

If there are times you don't feel love for who or what you've listed, that's okay. For example, maybe you recently got into an argument with a partner or had a bad day at your job, which lowers your affection ratings in these areas. It's normal for feelings of love to wax and wane. I still would encourage you to keep lower-intensity sparks of affection on your list. In Step 3, we can work on spotlighting them to see if that increases the rating.

Step 2: To start this second step, list your five categories in a single column along the left-hand side of another sheet of paper. Leave plenty of space between each category.

Now describe where, when, and how the sources you identified in Step 1 appear in your life. To keep this step manageable, you may only want to choose one source to explore in each category. Here are some questions that can guide you:

- How often does this source appear? Weekly? Daily?

- In what forms does it appear most often? Words, actions, or thoughts?

- Where am I most likely to encounter this source? At work? Home?

- How long do its sparks last?

- Would I want this source to be more present, or have a higher intensity of affection? If so, how might I make that happen?

Step 3: In this final step, you will spotlight some of the strongest examples of love from your map. I encourage you to start by picking a few with the highest intensity. Close your eyes and picture yourself coming into contact with those sparks. You could choose a recent example, such as a hug you received from someone you care about, or engaging in an activity you love. Alternatively, you could imagine a future moment of affection in any of the categories and how that might look.

As vividly as possible, picture all the details of that interaction or activity: your thoughts, feelings, sense of closeness, what was said, or any other kind of notable moment. You may want to look at a photograph, if you have one available, to bring out your loving thoughts and feelings more clearly.

Take note of the effects of opening this pathway to love. Do you feel more relaxed, happy, content, or hopeful? What thoughts are circulating now?

I invite you to capture some of those thoughts and put them somewhere you might easily see them again, perhaps on a sticky note or in your phone. Some points on your Affections Map may shine brightly and carry a considerable amount of love. If that's the case, great! It is also common to struggle with finding sources of love or activating them at different points in our lives.

In that case, your Affections Map can serve as a powerful reminder of your love's *desired* reach. You might realize you want to show more affection toward yourself, your children, or your coworkers. Or you may notice that the feeling of warmth fades quickly, as stressful thoughts or negative memories edge their way into your awareness. If so, you could then focus your practice around sustaining that warmth by thinking of more examples of loving expressions: words, actions, and gestures. Feel free to download the "Your Affections Map" worksheet at http://www.newharbinger.com/47858, if you like.

Another way to use your Affections Map is to transfer your sources of love into circles on a sheet of paper, so it looks more like an actual map. You can draw lines connecting the circles, thinking of the relationships between them—for example, love for family and nature may coincide when you take walks together.

Every time you look at your map, see if you can feel the full scope of your love's reach. Are there boundaries you would like to extend? Are there new paths you would like to create? What possibilities about yourself do your affections reveal?

The answers to these questions speak to your natural tendency to grow in positive directions, bringing us back full circle to the Flower Philosophy of Change. Love lies at the core of that philosophy.

When we love ourselves and others, we can grow. We want to try new things, be kind, express thanks, and celebrate strengths. In this way, love can help you reach your fullest potential as a human being, a state that psychologist Abraham Maslow (1987) called self-actualization. Over the past six weeks, you have been systematically working your way toward this state. We'll return to the idea of self-actualization in a bit.

But first, let's look at an example of an Affections Map from Faith, who describes how identifying love's pathways helped her feel more connected and joyful.

Faith's Story: A Vast Map of Affection

At sixty-four years old, Faith lives in ways that keep her energetic, centered, playful, and appreciative. She has many sources of love driving these positive feelings, clearly identified on her map. They include her son, husband, and friends. Faith also gets in touch with

*love in her role as a therapist when she witnesses her clients'
breakthroughs.*

*Her affection for life encompasses her dog Moxie, gardens and
trees, really good food, and snowstorms. For Faith, love's branches
extend through activities like walking, hiking, watching the sun rise,
and taking road trips.*

*Seeing her family and friends regularly keeps that ember of deep
caring burning brightly. In looking at her map, Faith also realized how
playing with Moxie brings back loving feelings from her childhood,
since she grew up with terriers. She found that this spark ignited an
even stronger love for her parents and siblings.*

*Visualizing parts of her map related to family made Faith feel
safe, comforted, and understood. "They ground my whole day," she
wrote. In addition to her love for family, Faith found herself feeling
more hopeful about the future when streaming get-togethers with
friends and recalling her clients' leaps of progress. As a result, she was
able to envision a world "where there is more love and affection by
people for one another."*

The Kindling Effect of Love

Because love is such a powerful positive emotion, you may notice a kindling effect, like Faith did, during the Affections Map exercise. We first
explored this "spread" effect of spotlighting in Week 1. Love just might be
the strongest kind of positivity-igniter.

To explore this effect firsthand, think of someone or something you
love. It could be someone you feel very close to, a family member or best
friend, or a creative activity that expresses a central part of who you are.
Watch what happens inside when you bring that image to mind.

There's a good chance it will light up positive thoughts, such as *I am someone who is capable of being loved* or *I have great meaning because I can do what I love.* Those thoughts usually have a great depth to them that can spark other positive emotions, like hope, contentment, and determination.

You may also find that coming into contact with love can raise your overall energy level during the day. It can help you feel more enthusiastic about work, daily chores, or socializing. You might notice you want to take better care of yourself, perhaps by exercising more, eating healthier foods, or practicing your *Happier You* skills.

Some of this spread effect may have to do with biochemical processes in the body. In loving states, our brains release dopamine and oxytocin, which increase pleasure, well-being, and a desire to bond with others (Love 2014). But there is a spiritual side to it as well.

Have you ever had the sense that love makes all things possible? When we are truly in touch with love, we are intimately connected with something greater than ourselves. You could think of it as a source of something divine, or a positive energy from which all life unfolds. By helping us connect to something benevolent and greater than ourselves, love gives us hope. And this is especially important when the world seems darkest.

There is a very practical side to all of this too. Whenever you tap into love, you are strengthening your resilience, your ability to bounce back from hardship. You can test this out for yourself.

The next time you catch yourself ruminating about a disappointment or a stressful event, turn to your Affections Map. Pick something from it, stream a moment related to it, and see if you notice a shift in how you feel.

Accessing love may soften that disappointment or ease the stress you feel, making it more manageable. You could ask yourself a key question to measure its effect: "Does what happened sting a bit less when I contact this source of love in my life?"

If the answer is no, or just a little bit, pick a different source from your map and try again. You might just need one with a higher affection-intensity level.

Let's stop here to check in. How good a grasp do you feel you have of love's sources and its spread effects? Remember that you can take as much time as you need working with different parts of your Affections Map, practicing kindling, and applying love to difficult moments.

If you would like to continue working on using love intentionally, the next exercise will guide you in taking that step. It will help you send love out into the world in ever-widening circles.

EXERCISE: Widening the Reach of Love

In Week 6, we turned to Buddhism to better understand the universal importance of kindness. In Buddhism, the ideas of love and kindness are often combined, and for good reason. We can greatly strengthen our capacity for loving-kindness when we consider what we have in common. As the Buddhist monk Thich Nhat Hanh (2014) so beautifully writes, we are all "made of stars" and "carry eternity inside."

How can this awareness of what we have in common with others guide us in widening our reach of love? How do we turn this awareness, regard, and love for others into a daily practice?

The act of thinking about our interconnectedness deepens our care for others. Unity, compassion, and love are intertwined. From this place, we become more capable of increasing love's range. We can extend it to those we don't know well or have difficulty with. Our embrace can even include entire cities or states.

This exercise will assist you in working with love across these different distances. You will not need any paper for it, just some quiet protected space where you can go inward without too many distractions. It would help to set aside about ten to fifteen minutes. For an audio version of this exercise, go to http://www.newharbinger.com/47858.

Step 1

In this first step, I invite you to draw forth feelings of unification through a series of self-statements and visualizations.

Self-Statements

After you read each statement, see if you can feel what that statement says. Closing your eyes might help make those feelings more powerful. If one statement in particular resonates with you, you can stay with that one, if you want.

- I am part of the human race, and so is everyone else.

- When I hurt, others hurt. When I feel joy, others feel joy.

- We all share the same Earth.

- When I care for others, I care for myself. When I care for myself, I am caring for others.

- Just as I hold loving intentions toward others, they hold the same intentions toward me.

Visualizations

After you read each visualization below, bring the image or sensations into your mind. Close your eyes if you think that will make the experience more vivid.

- Imagine watching the Earth from space. Sense how we all live on the same blue droplet in a vast ocean of darkness. Feel how we need each other, as a result.

- Watch the rise and fall of your chest as you breathe. With each breath in, picture everyone else on the planet breathing in at the same time. With each breath out, picture everyone else on the planet breathing out at the same time.

- Imagine everyone in the world stops what they are doing, including you. Picture that you all have a sudden awareness of the importance of every other person's presence and how special it is. You matter greatly to them, and they to you.

Step 2

Now that you have established a foundation of unity, you are ready to send loving thoughts and feelings outward. This part of the exercise is similar to the Stepladder Of Gratitude in Week 3. With each new level, you increase the distance that your love travels. The further out you go, the more difficult this may become. Try to complete the levels in order, but by all means, feel free to take a break or return to an earlier level if you run into any resistance.

Similar to Step 1, to increase the intensity of deep caring that you feel, you may want to read each level's instruction first and then follow that instruction with your eyes closed. Alternatively, you may prefer to listen to the available recording of this exercise.

The specific loving thoughts and feelings you project outward are up to you. However, some examples include *I am sending you understanding, warmth, and caring, I am opening my heart to you,* and *You are deserving of love.*

Level 1—With Ease

Think of someone you love with ease. Picture them as clearly as possible in your mind. Once you feel connected to them, send them loving thoughts and feelings.

Level 2—Toward the Unfamiliar

Now think of someone you don't know that well. It could be someone from your job, a member of a group you are part of, a relative you don't often see, or someone you tend to interact with at a surface level. Picture them as clearly as possible in your mind. Once you have them in mind, send them loving thoughts and feelings.

Level 3—With Tension

Turn your mind now toward someone with whom you have felt some tension. Perhaps it was someone you argued with recently, or who wronged you in some way. Picture them as clearly as possible in your mind. Once you do, as best you can, send them loving thoughts and feelings.

Level 4—By Location

Now I invite you to widen the focus of your loving thoughts and feelings to include many other people. Begin by sending those thoughts and feelings to everyone in your community or neighborhood. Pause to imagine your thoughts and feelings being received.

When you are ready, see if you can expand that circle to include everyone in your state or country. Pause to allow your loving thoughts and feelings to sweep across everyone there. When you are ready, expand your circle again to include the entire world. Send loving thoughts and feelings to everyone on Earth. Pause to appreciate the warmth and scope of that.

Level 5—Toward Yourself

As a last step, send loving thoughts and feelings to yourself. Here you want to bring your loving embrace back to a single focus: you. Know that you are as deserving of these loving thoughts and feelings as anyone else you have sent them to.

Let's stop to see how that went. How did sending love in this way make you feel? As with your Affections Map, you may have noticed feeling more physically relaxed, more open to others, or more energetic. What positive thoughts did you catch? They might have included thoughts of thankfulness, lightness, or strengths.

Did you feel an urge to reach out to the person you were focusing on? If so, wonderful! I would encourage you to turn that desire into action.

At the community or global level, you may have felt inspired to show love in a way that benefits humankind, perhaps by getting involved in a humanitarian cause like fighting climate change. This could lead to actions like volunteering or joining a Facebook group with a similar interest.

Now let's explore the opposite effect. Did you get stuck anywhere?

It would be normal, for example, to find that anger or frustration toward someone in your life blocked your expression of caring. You might also have found Level 4 challenging as a result of negative systemic forces in the world, like racism, poverty, or political strife—forces that are so vast it can be hard to imagine what any one individual can do about them. In addition, some people have trouble loving themselves, as a result of frequent self-criticism or low self-worth.

If you encountered any of these obstacles, I would ask that you show yourself compassion by not criticizing your effort. Widening the reach of love in a lasting way often takes repetition and commitment. It could require many weeks, if not years, of practice, and a sustained commitment to returning to the practice when you find you've fallen out of the habit.

Psychologist and meditator Steven Schwartzberg (2016) explains that sending someone love *no matter what* represents some of the toughest internal work you can do. It often requires suspending judgment, finding forgiveness, and lowering your defenses. So I encourage you to be patient and persistent while you build your capacity for more encompassing feelings of love.

To make the exercise more manageable, you might want to practice one level per day and not move on until you feel sufficient ease in that level's "love send." A good sign you are ready to move on to the next level is if you don't sense any friction as you send your internal messages of deep caring out into the world.

It may also help to keep in mind the reasons *why* you want to widen the reach of love through this work. I can think of two:

- It can make your inner life softer, more peaceful, and more understanding.

- It can turn the world around you into a more loving place, especially when you can translate those thoughts and feelings into actions.

Adina's example of expanding love's boundaries shows the strong positive effect this exercise can have on social, spiritual, and appreciative dimensions of self.

Adina's Story: Sending Love Outward

Adina is a preschool teacher and mom who deeply values family, love, and acceptance. Her process of directing love outward began with her husband as the focal point, which stirred up feelings of gratitude for his tireless work in supporting their family.

Adina then extended her range to include a college student who had worked in her preschool class, now starting graduate school in a new town. She sent "good vibes" and supportive thoughts to her while also appreciating the student's commitment, intelligence, and bravery.

At the next level, Adina sent love to someone she felt frustrated with for not upholding values important in the educational field. And she found that, instead of feeling anger, she wanted positive things for this person, like inspiration, courage, growth, and open-mindedness.

Finally, expanding love to its widest reach, Adina focused on the world as a whole, sending everyone on Earth peace and compassion. She immediately felt the deep importance of spreading love and understanding in this way among all people. She described a kind of spiritual happiness that emerged, writing, "I'm so glad my thoughts are out in the universe, heading to those I thought about."

In this exercise, Adina struggled most with sending love to herself, which is not uncommon as we contend with the difficulties of life and negative forces in the world around us. It is worth paying special attention to this challenge as we move ahead.

Loving Yourself

All of the skills you have been practicing so far in A Happier You, from catching positive events to activating kindness, are ways in which you are showing yourself love. By caring deeply for your inner and outer worlds in these ways, you are saying, I am worth feeling good every day, no matter what. Loving yourself unconditionally means continuing to feel affection for who you are despite your mistakes, your down days, and your struggles.

The conditions may not always be ideal. You may face depression, loss, trauma, sickness, or other negative life events. You could hit rough patches in work, family, friendships, creativity, and finances. You might stumble in your discipline around diet and exercise, or lose your composure with your children when stressed. Loving yourself is a commitment you can honor through all of it. It is the recognition that you are learning, that you have courage, that you are worth the effort, and that you have value even when you mess up or fail.

Do you feel ready to make that commitment now? Or maybe you have already made it by traveling across these weeks of the Happier You program. Either way, you might imagine saying to yourself, Even though I am not at my personal best today, I will keep faith in who I am and my potential. This "no matter what" mantra can help you wake up the next day and try again.

As Abraham Maslow (1987) and the flower philosophy tell us, we naturally climb toward peak states of well-being if we have the right conditions around us. Loving yourself is part of creating those right conditions. To self-actualize, as Maslow puts it, we need to love ourselves at every point along the way. In other words, we need to become our own nurturers.

I don't mean this in an egotistical way. None of it involves bragging or putting yourself above others. From a Happier You perspective, you love yourself by carrying a quiet appreciation for who you are, feeling compassion for your difficulties, and spotlighting your best qualities so you can stay conscious of them and cultivate them.

In thinking about this kind of self-love, here are some points worth highlighting:

- Any kind of self-care is a form of love, and you deserve it no matter what.

- Loving yourself is a commitment that can guide your thoughts and actions in good times and bad.

- In loving yourself, you are believing in your potential.

- Deeply caring for who you are can get easier with practice.

This next exercise is designed to give you that practice. It will show you ways to love yourself *just as you are* in this moment. It will help you feel affection through many parts of your being. You will also explore how love can continue to drive your personal transformation in the days and weeks to come.

EXERCISE: Loving Yourself Fully

This exercise is based on the idea that you can always find a way to deeply care for yourself. You will start from a place of self-acceptance and then reaffirm a commitment to loving yourself. From there, you will go on to identify examples of that love in many areas of life. Finally, you will develop a vision for how you can love yourself more fully in the future.

I suggest you have a sheet or two of paper and ten to fifteen minutes of time to yourself. If any step feels too difficult, or doesn't yield much, simply move on to the next step or come back to the exercise later.

Step 1: Loving yourself often begins with acceptance. So let's take a moment to step into that meadow. Wherever you are emotionally, physically, and socially right now is okay. Within this place of tranquil observation, try to affirm a commitment to loving yourself.

You could say or think something like *I will love myself no matter what, even during the toughest of times.* I encourage you to use your own words to make this commitment as powerful and genuine as possible.

Sometimes this first step requires forgiving yourself for mistakes, shortcomings, or problems. Self-forgiveness does not always come easily, so you may need to return to this step repeatedly during the week.

Step 2: Now I would ask that you open the door to loving yourself in the present moment, or in the very recent past. These questions can get you started:

- What do I love about myself right now, in this very moment?

- Is there something I said or did today that could be a reason for affection?

The answers could be big or small reasons related to any of the areas we have covered in *A Happier You.* Examples include noticing a relationship strength, recognizing an act of kindness you performed, being able to laugh at a stressful moment, or spending time at a gratitude spot. There are so many possibilities.

As best you can, allow the deep caring that comes from those answers to resonate through you. Notice any positive changes around how you feel in your body. For instance, do you feel a warmth in your chest, or a deeper sense of relaxation?

Step 3: In this step, you will work to channel love through the many parts of who you are. These parts correspond to the seven dimensions of wellness we've talked about before. For example, you may love your social self today because you made someone laugh, or your spiritual self if you have been praying or attending religious services. You may have gone above and beyond on your job recently, leading you to feel love for your work ethic.

To intensify the effect of this step, see if you can bring these reasons to mind one after the other: *I love my social self because... I love my creative self because... I love my physical self because...* If nothing comes to mind in one of the categories, you could move on to the next one and come back at a later time.

Step 4: This last step involves looking toward the future for ways that you could love yourself more. Do you want to take better care of your body, mind, or spirit? If so, how? You might see opportunities to get more sleep, eat a healthier diet, exercise more regularly, or pace your workday. Loving yourself more fully may center around emotional self-care.

Think back to each of the Core Positivity Practices we have covered across the past six weeks: positive events, successes and strengths, gratitude, lightness, enjoyable and meaningful activities, and kindness.

In the coming week, is there one area in particular that you want to love yourself through? If so, how might you do that? Write down a couple ideas for a plan. It may involve returning to a previous week's exercise. You might want to set aside more time to stream the good moments of your day. It could be as simple as making yourself a nice meal, or spending time with a good friend.

By loving yourself more fully through this exercise, you will likely find a greater depth of love for others. Let's pause here to look at that connection.

How much warmth and value do you feel for yourself after trying this exercise? Do you notice any changes in how you interact with others? Are you kinder or more patient?

If you have the energy and time for only one step in this exercise, I would recommend Step 2. Checking in, every day, about what you love about yourself can have a positive emotion kindling effect, like we talked about earlier. Keep looking out for those signposts. Remember too that any time you have spent reading this book shows how much you believe in your importance and potential.

A Final Reflection Point

In this final week of A *Happier You*, you have taken a deep dive into the currents of love that drive positivity. When you love yourself and others, you open the doors to peace and happiness. You become better able to bounce back from difficulties. You also move closer to your best possible self and a best possible world.

The key Core Positivity Practices this week are:

- Gaining a better awareness of who and what you have affection for

- Strengthening the intensity and effects of love's sources in your life

- Expanding the reach of loving thoughts and feelings

- Deepening love for yourself

I recognize that loving yourself and others can at times feel challenging, especially if you don't feel cared for in return. That's why I want to emphasize taking your time as you integrate these exercises into your life:

- Your Affections Map

- Widening the Reach of Love

- Loving Yourself Fully

Linger as long as you need to on their individual steps. If they feel too difficult, you could always return to another part of A *Happier You* and work on those skills instead.

As we find ourselves here together at the end of this seven-week journey, I want to commend you on reaching this self-care milestone! You are now equipped with a full range of positivity tools to reduce negative thinking, spark positive feelings, and build resilience. You now know specific ways to:

- Catch and magnify positive events

- Spotlight successes and personal strengths

- Cultivate gratitude

- Find laughter and playfulness

- Fill your weeks with enjoyable and meaningful activities

- Live with kindness

- Expand the intensity and reach of love

It may be best to view these past seven weeks as a starting point—the beginning of an enduring lifestyle of positivity. You will likely need to continue practicing your Core Positivity skills to keep them sharp.

In that spirit, this book could act as your "charging station." You can come back to it when your positivity levels are low, when you need reminders of your strengths, or to review the step-by-step approach to exercises in each positivity area. A bonus chapter, "Full Spectrum Happiness," is also available on New Harbinger's website that offers additional ways to integrate these practice areas into your day-to-day life. Visit http://www .newharbinger.com/47858 to download it.

It is no small feat to have finished this journey. You have dedicated seven weeks to revealing your best self and celebrating the most rewarding parts of life. You have established a commitment to positive living—to thinking, feeling, and acting in ways that make life's stressful moments more bearable.

This is a positive way of being in the world, and perhaps very different from the one that has felt most familiar up until now. Your new positivity habits should grow stronger over time. One way to help that growth is to share these habits with others. You may not know it, but you are now a *Happier You* teacher, capable of modeling positive ways of responding to whatever arises in life and inevitably inspiring others around you to do the same. And more than simply being a better responder, you have become proactive in creating a daily foundation for feeling good.

Although you may encounter some bumps along the way, and we all do, this way of being can stay with you for the rest of your life, if you so choose. You can think of yourself as a flower that is determined to bloom *no matter what*. By practicing these skills, you are doing amazing things with the gift of life, strengthening its most positive guiding forces—and that helps all of us lead happier lives.

References

Amaro, L. M. 2017. "Dyadic Effects of Gratitude on Burden, Conflict, and Contribution in the Family Caregiver and Sibling Relationship." *Journal of Applied Communication Research* 45 (1): 61–78.

Aspy, D. J., and M. Proeve. 2017. "Mindfulness and Loving-Kindness Meditation: Effects on Connectedness to Humanity and to the Natural World. *Psychological Reports* 120: 102–117.

Beechler, M. P. 2018. "Revisiting the Egoism-Altruism Debate: Effects of Contextual Cues on Empathy, Oneness, and Helping Intentions." *North American Journal of Psychology* 20: 23–36.

Bennett, M. P., and C. Lengacher. 2009. "Humor and Laughter May Influence Health IV. Humor and Immune Function." *Evidence-Based Complementary Alternative Medicine* 6: 159–164.

Bernard, B. P., R. J. Driscoll, M. Kitt, C. A. West, and S. W. Tak. 2006. "Health Hazard Evaluation of Police Officers and Firefighters after Hurricane Katrina–New Orleans, Louisiana, October 17–28 and November 30–December 5, 2005." *Morbidity and Mortality Weekly Report* 55: 456–458.

Binfet, J. T., and J. Whitehead. 2019. "The Effect of Engagement in a Kindness Intervention on Adolescents' Well-Being: A Randomized Controlled Trial. *International Journal of Emotional Education* 11: 33–49.

Cousins, N. 1979. *Anatomy of an Illness as Perceived by the Patient: Reflections on Healing and Regeneration.* New York: W. W. Norton.

Csikszentmihalyi, M. 2008. *Flow: The Psychology of Optimal Experience.* New York: Harper and Row.

Dickens, L. R. 2017. "Using Gratitude to Promote Positive Change: A Series of Meta-Analyses Investigating the Effectiveness of Gratitude Interventions." *Basic and Applied Social Psychology* 39: 193–208.

Feldman, D. B., K. L. Rand, and K. Kahle-Wrobleski. 2009. "Hope and Goal Attainment: Testing a Basic Prediction of Hope Theory." *Journal of Social and Clinical Psychology* 28: 479–497.

Frankl, V. E. 1962. *Man's Search for Meaning: An Introduction to Logotherapy*. Translated by Ilse Lasch. New York: Simon and Schuster.

Fredman Stein, K., W. L. Morys-Carter, and L. Hinkley. 2018. "Rumination and Impaired Prospective Memory." *Journal of General Psychology* 145: 266–279.

Fredrickson, B. L. 2001. "The Role of Positive Emotions in Positive Psychology: The Broaden-and-Build Theory of Positive Emotions." *American Psychologist* 56: 218–226.

Gutsol, O. 2019. *108 Buddhist Parables and Stories*. Self-published.

Hanh, T. N. 2014. *How to Love*. Berkeley, CA: Parallax Press.

Hendriks, T., M. Schotanus-Dijkstra, A. Hassankhan, J. de Jong, and E. Bohlmeijer. 2020. "The Efficacy of Multi-Component Positive Psychology Interventions: A Systematic Review and Meta-Analysis of Randomized Controlled Trials." *Journal of Happiness Studies* 21: 357–390.

Howes, C. 2009. "Friendship in Early Childhood." In *Handbook of Peer Interactions, Relationships, and Groups*, edited by K. H. Rubin, W. M. Bukowski, and B. Laursen, 180–194. New York: Guilford Press.

Kabat-Zinn, J. 2013. *Full Catastrophe Living: Using the Wisdom of Your Body and Mind to Face Stress, Pain, and Illness*. New York: Bantam Books.

Kabat-Zinn, J. 1994. *Wherever You Go, There You Are: Mindfulness Meditation in Everyday Life*. New York: Hyperion.

Kashdan, T. B., J. Yarbro, P. E. McKnight, and J. B. Nezlek. 2014. "Laughter with Someone Else Leads to Future Social Rewards: Temporal Change Using Experience Sampling Methodology." *Personality and Individual Differences* 58: 15–19.

Kline, L. W. 1907. "The Psychology of Humor." *The American Journal of Psychology* 18: 421–441.

Kurtz, L. E. and S. B. Algoe. 2015. "Putting Laughter in Context: Shared Laughter as Behavioral Indicator of Relationship Well-Being." *Personal Relationships* 22: 573–590.

Long, M. "The Long Run." Filmed November 2011. Talks at Google video, 53 minutes. Posted November 2011. https://www.youtube.com/watch?v=hCIdQNvcLT0.

Love, T. M. 2014. "Oxytocin, Motivation, and the Role of Dopamine." *Pharmacology, Biochemistry, and Behavior* 119: 49–60.

Manninen, S., L. Tuominen, R. I. Dunbar, T. Karjalainen, J. Hirvonen, E. Arponen, R. Hari, I. P. Jääskeläinen, M. Sams, and L. Nummenmaa. 2017. "Social Laughter Triggers Endogenous Opioid Release in Humans." *The Journal of Neuroscience: The Official Journal of the Society for Neuroscience* 37: 6125–6131.

Martínez-Hernáez, A., N. Carceller-Maicas, S. M. DiGiacomo, and S. Ariste. 2016. "Social Support and Gender Differences in Coping with Depression Among Emerging Adults: A Mixed-Methods Study." *Child and Adolescent Psychiatry and Mental Health* 10. Accessed July 20, 2020. https://capmh.biomedcentral.com/articles/10.1186/s13034-015 -0088-x.

Maslow, A. H. 1987. *Motivation and Personality*. 3rd edition. New York: Harper and Row Publishers.

McCanlies, E. C., J. K. Gu, M. E. Andrew, and J. M. Violanti. 2018. "The Effect of Social Support, Gratitude, Resilience, and Satisfaction with Life on Depressive Symptoms Among Police Officers Following Hurricane Katrina." *International Journal of Social Psychiatry* 64: 63–72.

Miller, W. R., J. C'de Baca, and P. L. Matthews. 2001. "Personal Values Card Sort." Accessed August 3, 2020. www.motivationalinterviewing. org/sites/default/files/valuescardsort_0.pdf.

Navarro, J. L., and Tudge, J. R. H. 2020. "What Is Gratitude? Ingratitude Provides the Answer." *Human Development* 64 (2): 83–96.

Neff, K. D. 2003. "Self-Compassion Scale." *Self and Identity* 2: 223–250.

Nohlen, H. U., F. van Harreveld, and W. A. Cunningham. 2019. "Social Evaluations Under Conflict: Negative Judgments of Conflicting Information Are Easier than Positive Judgments." *Social Cognitive and Affective Neuroscience* 14: 709–718.

North, A. C., M. Tarrant, and D. J. Hargreaves. 2004. "The Effects of Music on Helping Behavior: A Field Study." *Environment and Behavior* 36: 266–275

Nwokah, E. E., H. C. Hsu, O. Dobrowolska, and A. Fogel. 1994. "The Development of Laughter in Mother-Infant Communication: Timing Parameters and Temporal Sequences." *Infant Behavior and Development* 17: 23–35.

Park, Y., E. A. Impett, G. MacDonald, and E. P. Lemay. 2019. "Saying 'Thank You': Partners' Expressions of Gratitude Protect Relationship Satisfaction and Commitment from the Harmful Effects of Attachment Insecurity." *Journal of Personality and Social Psychology* 117: 773–806.

Peterson, C. and M. E. P. Seligman. (2004). *Character Strengths and Virtues: A Handbook and Classification.* Washington, D.C.: American Psychological Association; Oxford University Press.

Phale, M., and D. Korgaonkar. 2008. "Pharmacology of Learning and Memory." *The Internet Journal of Pharmacology* 7. Accessed August 3, 2020. https://ispub.com/IJPHARM/7/1/12011.

Provine, R. R. 2000. *Laughter: A Scientific Investigation.* New York: Viking.

Rowland, L., and O. S. Curry. 2019. "A Range of Kindness Activities Boost Happiness." *Journal of Social Psychology* 159: 340–343.

Sakurada, K., K. Tsuneo, M. Watanabe, K. Ishizawa, Y. Ueno, H. Yamashita, and T. Kayama. 2019. "Associations of Frequency of Laughter with Risk of All-Cause Mortality and Cardiovascular Disease Incidence in a General Population: Findings from the Yamagata Study." *Journal of Epidemiology* 30: 188–193.

Schmitt, A., M. M. Gielnik, and S. Seibel. 2018. "When and How Does Anger during Goal Pursuit Relate to Goal Achievement? The Roles of Persistence and Action Planning." *Motivation and Emotion* 43: 205–217.

Schwartz, C. E., P. M. Keyl, J. P. Marcum, and R. Bode. 2009. "Helping Others Shows Differential Benefits on Health and Well-Being for Male and Female Teens." *Journal of Happiness Studies* 10: 431–448.

Schwartzberg, S. 2016. "The Two Tiers of Buddhist Loving-Kindness Practice." *Huffington Post*, March 18, 2016. Accessed July 18, 2020. http://www.huffpost.com/entry/the-two-tiers-of-buddhist_b_9488502.

Segal, Z. V., J. M. Williams, and J. D. Teasdale. 2013. *Mindfulness-Based Cognitive Therapy for Depression.* 2nd edition. New York: Guilford Press.

Seligman, M. E. P. 2012. *Flourish: A Visionary Understanding of Happiness and Well-Being*. New York: Simon and Schuster.

Strack, J., F. Esteves, P. Lopes, and P. Fernandez-Berrocal. 2017. "Must We Suffer to Succeed?: When Anxiety Boosts Motivation and Performance." *Journal of Individual Differences* 38: 113–124.

Substance Abuse and Mental Health Services Administration. 2016. "Creating a Healthier Life: A Step-by-Step Guide to Wellness." Accessed October 15, 2019. https://store.samhsa.gov/product/Creating -a-Healthier-Life-/SMA16-4958.

Swarbrick, M. 2006. "A Wellness Approach." *Psychiatric Rehabilitation Journal* 29: 311–314.

Trussler, M., and S. Soroka. 2014. "Consumer Demand for Cynical and Negative News Frames." *International Journal of Press/Politics*, 19: 360–379.

Veerapa, E., P. Grandgenevre, M. El Fayoumi, B. Vinnac, O. Haelewyn, S. Szaffarczyk, G. Vaiva, and F. D'Hondt. 2020. "Attentional Bias Towards Negative Stimuli in Healthy Individuals and the Effects of Trait Anxiety." *Scientific Reports* 10, 11826.

Westburg, N. G. 2003. "Hope, Laughter, and Humor in Residents and Staff at an Assisted Living Facility." *Journal of Mental Health Counseling* 25: 16–32.

Wildgruber, D., D. P. Szameitat, T. Ethofer, C. Brück, K. Alter, W. Grodd, and B. Kreifelts. 2013. "Different Types of Laughter Modulate Connectivity within Distinct Parts of the Laughter Perception Network." *PLoS ONE* 8: 1–15.

Zawadzki, M. J., M. J. Sliwinski, and J. M. Smyth. 2018. "Perseverative Cognitions and Stress Exposure: Comparing Relationships with Psychological Health Across a Diverse Adult Sample." *Annals of Behavioral Medicine* 52: 1060–1072.

Zhao, J., H. Yin, G. Zhang, G. Li, B. Shang, C. Wang, and L. Chen. 2019. "A Meta-Analysis of Randomized Controlled Trials of Laughter and Humour Interventions on Depression, Anxiety, and Sleep Quality in Adults." *Journal of Advanced Nursing* 75: 2435–2448.

Scott Glassman, PsyD, is a licensed psychologist, and clinical associate professor at the Philadelphia College of Osteopathic Medicine. Glassman's program, A Happier You®, was featured on National Public Radio (NPR) and CBS News through national syndication. He has appeared on SiriusXM's *Doctor Radio* to discuss his work on happiness. Additionally, Glassman is a contributing psychology and health writer for *The Philadelphia Inquirer* and www.philly.com.

ABOUT US

Founded by psychologist Matthew McKay and Patrick Fanning, New Harbinger has published books that promote wellness in mind, body, and spirit for more than forty-five years.

Our proven-effective self-help books and pioneering workbooks help readers of all ages and backgrounds make positive lifestyle changes, improve mental health and well-being, and achieve meaningful personal growth. In addition, our spirituality books offer profound guidance for deepening awareness and cultivating healing, self-discovery, and fulfillment.

New Harbinger is proud to be an independent and employee-owned company, publishing books that reflect its core values of integrity, innovation, commitment, sustainability, compassion, and trust. Written by leaders in the field and recommended by therapists worldwide, New Harbinger books are practical, reliable, and provide real tools for real change.

 **newharbinger**publications

MORE BOOKS from
NEW HARBINGER PUBLICATIONS

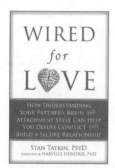

WIRED FOR LOVE

How Understanding Your Partner's Brain and Attachment Style Can Help You Defuse Conflict and Build a Secure Relationship

978-1608820580 / US $17.95

ADULT CHILDREN OF EMOTIONALLY IMMATURE PARENTS

How to Heal from Distant, Rejecting, or Self-Involved Parents

978-1626251700 / US $18.95

ACT DAILY JOURNAL

Get Unstuck and Live Fully with Acceptance and Commitment Therapy

978-1684037377 / US $18.95

THE UNTETHERED SOUL

The Journey Beyond Yourself

978-1-572245372 / US $18.95

THE LITTLE BOOK OF BIG CHANGE

The No-Willpower Approach to Breaking Any Habit

978-1626252301 / US $16.95

FUEL YOUR BRAIN, NOT YOUR ANXIETY

Stop the Cycle of Worry, Fatigue, and Sugar Cravings with Simple Protein-Rich Foods

978-1684036233 / US $21.95

Did you know there are free tools you can download for this book?

Free tools are things like **worksheets, guided meditation exercises**, and **more** that will help you get the most out of your book.

You can download free tools for this book—whether you bought or borrowed it, in any format, from any source— from the **New Harbinger** website. All you need is a NewHarbinger.com account. Just use the URL provided in this book to view the free tools that are available for it. Then, click on the "download" button for the free tool you want, and follow the prompts that appear to log in to your NewHarbinger.com account and download the material.

You can also save the free tools for this book to your **Free Tools Library** so you can access them again anytime, just by logging in to your account! Just look for this button on the book's free tools page:

+ save this to my
free tools library

If you need help accessing or downloading free tools, visit **newharbinger.com/faq** or contact us at customerservice@newharbinger.com.

CELEBRATING
40 YEARS